THE GOOD PSYCHOLOGIST

The Good Psychologist insists on preserving an optimum clinical distance. He's always aware that the unshakeable conviction that disaster is approaching has become the real disaster in the lives of the anxious. But take a closer look at the Good Psychologist. Who is that waving to him seductively from his past? What's beckoning him to rekindle extinguished hopes for the future? As the shell of his detachment begins to crack, he finds himself pulled where the boundaries between professional and personal are dangerously blurring.

NOAM SHPANCER

THE GOOD PSYCHOLOGIST

Complete and Unabridged

ULVERSCROFT
Leicester

First published in Great Britain in 2011 by
Abacus
An imprint of
Little, Brown Book Group, London

First Large Print Edition
published 2012
by arrangement with
Little, Brown Book Group
An Hachette UK Company, London

British Library CIP Data

Shpancer, Noam.
   The good psychologist.
   1. Psychologists- -Fiction.
   2. Large type books.
   I. Title
   892.4'37–dc23

   ISBN 978–1–4448–1355–5

Published by
F. A. Thorpe (Publishing)
Anstey, Leicestershire

Set by Words & Graphics Ltd.
Anstey, Leicestershire
Printed and bound in Great Britain by
T. J. International Ltd., Padstow, Cornwall

This book is printed on acid-free paper

For Mia Lewis

Look out child, it look like something be coming
It be coming the long way around
Coming the long way around

Chris Whitley, 'Long Way Around'

The psychologist sits in his small office, rests his elbows on his desk, buries his face in his hands and wishes that his four o'clock won't show up. He doesn't usually take appointments after three in the afternoon. But he has decided to deviate from his usual routine for her. A small concession because she works late and sleeps late and can only make it in the late afternoon, that's what she said over the phone. Her voice, cheerless and scattered like a motel room abandoned in haste, raised a vague curiosity in him. Small concessions, he likes to tell his clients, are like pocket change: it's what most of us have to work with, in the final analysis. Our small change is our daily habits and routines, our everyday, and the measure of one's life emerges, in the final analysis, from the sum of these everydays.

His daily routine, for example, is simple and straightforward. He wakes up early each morning in his small apartment, showers and gets dressed. The apartment is deliberately dark. Tall wooden shelves, heavy with books, line the living room walls. In the past, during his days of searching and wandering, he used

1

to immerse himself in these books. He has long since tired, or, to his mind, settled down. But still he finds solace in these paper bricks that line the walls, as if they were holding up the roof.

After he dresses he goes to the kitchen, makes himself a cup of tea and sits down to read the paper. Assorted objects — gifts and souvenirs given to him by his clients over the years — are strewn around the kitchen. Above the small, square table hangs a framed print of Bonnard's *Table Set in a Garden*, a gift from a former client, a borderline cellist who appeared on his lawn one night and set her hair on fire. You're a cockroach, she yelled at him then, a cockroach. If I step on you, you'll be squashed. He likes to stare at the picture: a table set among the trees, one chair, a bottle of wine, and yellow light spilling through the branches, startlingly alive.

The decorated brass plate on the table was given to him by another client, a travel agent with long braids, after he helped her get over an ex-boyfriend. When he asked her to describe a memory that could represent their relationship, she told him how the boyfriend taught her to brush her teeth while listening to the radio. Brush from the beginning of a song until it ends, the boyfriend said; that's how you'll know you have brushed for three minutes, as you should. And then she cried.

The colorful earthenware mug he holds in his hands was given to him by a client whose name he has forgotten, an artist who said, you've helped me a lot, and asked if she could leave him a small gift, and stood for a second at the door on her way out and whispered, my husband beats me, and left and did not return.

The blue towel with which he dries his hands was given to him by an obsessive-compulsive client who used to wash every part of her body with its own towel, sixteen towels per shower, and then had to wash each towel separately six times and then wash her hands six times in the sink. The sight of an errant air bubble in the hand soap bottle would compel her to wrap the bottle in a brown bag and toss it in the trash and run to the store to buy another.

In a kitchen cabinet stands an old half-empty bottle of brandy given to him years ago by a client who later killed himself like this: he sat in the empty bathtub and cut his left wrist with a butcher knife. Then he tried to slash his right wrist but failed. He didn't give up. He put the knife between his knees and sawed his right wrist, up and down. On a rutted pizza box in the living room he had scribbled a will: *Please cremate* my body. *Put my ashes in a trash can. Thank you.*

By now, the psychologist believes he has solved most of the problems of daily existence. He lives on a quiet, shaded street. His neighbors are busy with their own lives. His apartment is pleasant. The refrigerator is full and hums with satisfaction. The psychologist does his clinical work judiciously, between ten in the morning and three in the afternoon, and he compensates for the lost income by teaching an evening class every semester at the local college.

The psychologist has not yet solved the problem of sex. There are, to be sure, gauzy late night shows on cable. There are, too, groaning online sites. In the dresser hides an old beat-up DVD from the *Better Sex* series that he used years ago in his Human Sexuality course. The students giggled at the sight of several poor couples (*real people, not actors*, said the enclosed brochure) struggling to appear nonchalant and natural in front of the camera. But the psychologist finds fast relief, and a certain gratification, at the sight of one of the participants, a gloomy, dark-haired and sharp-nosed woman who stars, along with her mustachioed partner, in the 'Mutual Masturbation Techniques' chapter.

Beyond that there's Nina, or at least the memory of Nina, the hope of her.

Every day he drives to the Center for Anxiety Disorders — two small rooms on the ground floor of a building that was once a cheap motel and then abandoned. Over time it sprouted several businesses: an insurance company, an investment office, a travel agency, a photography store. Across the street, on the bank of the murky river that runs through the city, a new mall is being built. The noisy cacophony of trucks, cranes and tractors seeps through his office walls like the commotion from a children's playground. Across the narrow parking lot cars constantly fill the recently opened car wash. Sometimes he gazes from his office window at this daily parade, and sad, sweet music rises in him, like longing, at the sight of this attentive cleaning, the care with which soft towels and soft eyes caress the hoods, hubcaps, and bumpers.

The traffic had slowed to a crawl this morning on his way to work. *No Answer*, declared the bumper sticker on the back of the car that cut in front of him suddenly. Idiot, he cursed at the driver, a skinny, bald-headed guy whose elbow poked out of

5

his car's window like a reddish nose, and immediately he smiled to himself and forgave. Here's another example of the fundamental attribution error, he'll say later in class: You're waiting at the traffic light, perhaps, in a hurry to get somewhere; the light changes to green and the driver in front of you doesn't move. Immediately you call that driver an idiot and attribute to him all manner of terminal stupidity and rottenness of character. The next day you're at the light, first in line this time, but this time you're in no hurry and therefore humming with the radio and deep in thought. The light changes, and the driver behind you honks his horn. You turn around and call that driver — Idiot! Well? It turns out that, usually, neither you nor he are idiots. Both of you are but kindly, decent folk. The context, the situation determines our actions. He who wants to figure out human behavior should examine the circumstances before plunging into personality dissections — risky operations that usually fail and kill the patient, if there is a patient, if such personality dissections are not themselves the disease.

No Answer. That driver, an idiot or just absentminded, has already disappeared in traffic, but his sticker's announcement continues to gnaw at the psychologist's mind. He takes exception to all these bumper stickers, the jewelry and printed T-shirts, the tattoos with Chinese letters of obscure meaning. Ostensibly all these branding gestures are rooted in an attempt to assert one's identity and individuality, to escape a kind of annihilating anonymity. But the entire effort seems childish to him, exhausting, essentially anxious, and, in the final analysis, futile. The everyday is often seen as a punishment, an oppression against which one is supposed to rebel and rage; break and overthrow it with ceremonies and celebrations; delay it with speeches and exclamation points and parties and noise; cover it up in thick layers of makeup, mountains of words, loud music, and piles of food. The psychologist, however, finds comfort in the quiet murmur of the city's daily flow, the hushed rumbling of conversation that can be understood even without listening. The psychologist prefers the quiet, gray anonymity of the kind the city lavishes kindly on its inhabitants. All these escape efforts, the hassle of planning elaborate meals and dressing up, the compulsive marking of assorted special occasions, all these are suspect in his eyes. It is, after all, in those very special moments that the everyday stubbornly rises, slippery as smoke, seeps in and latches onto consciousness. In a room

7

filled with the scent of fresh love an ugly fly is always buzzing. Sand invades, sticky and malevolent, between the thighs of the lovers on the beach at sunset. The food cart squeals its tuneless song into the patient's hospital room, slices the doctor's speech somewhere between the *sorry* and the *cancer*. And here's a dwindling roll of toilet paper, a missing set of keys, a speck of sauce splashed unknowingly on the chin, dirty dishes in the sink, mud on the heels of the shoes. The psychologist has long ago surrendered to the everyday. He likens it to a wide and fast river, silent and strong, at once moving and still. Perhaps a total acceptance of this continuous prosaic moment, he thinks, allows one to truly transcend it, to arrive at what may lie beyond.

And still the bumper sticker issue rankles him. Surely there are some answers, somewhere. And beyond this, jewelry can be taken off and T-shirts changed and tattoos covered up. But a bumper sticker on a car is like a frozen facial expression, an irremovable mask, permanently fixed in place. And here's the paradox, he thinks: that sharp-elbowed baldy surely put the sticker on his bumper as a gesture of life, of giddiness, or as a sort of railing against diminishment, against erasure; an effort to sharpen his definition in the world. But the lack of response to shifting circumstances is an attribute of death. Thus the bumper sticker — a frozen smile on a corpse now flowing down the asphalt river — is, by definition, an emblem of demise, an epitaph.

You get to death from everywhere, Nina will quip when he'll tell her about his day on the phone later that evening.

Not just me, all of us.

Yes, she'll say, all of us, but not here. Not now. Isn't it you who likes to tell your clients how important it is to live in the here and now? Isn't it your speech that all fears emerge from projecting backward — what have I done? Or forward — what am I going to do? Isn't that your speech?

You're not my client.

So what am I to you?

It is being investigated. We're examining it.

Most of the clients at the Center for Anxiety Disorders share a certain look, a presence at once extinguished and buzzing. Their breathing is heavy, effortful and disorganized. Their eyes scan random magazines, retaining nothing. Their hands clasp the arms of their chairs as if a countdown has just begun at the end of which they will be launched into space in a terrifying heave. The psychologist is used to the haunted looks in the waiting room at all hours, the squashing of tissue paper, the wriggling fingers, and the terrified yawns. Still, when he entered the waiting room a week ago, exactly at four o'clock, he was taken aback by the sight of her. She was pale and slight like a refugee. Urban war paint was splashed over her face — black mascara, red lipstick. She stood up to greet him, fumbled forward on tall, clear heels. She did not look into his eyes but hung her gaze around his neck like a childish hug. He introduced himself and led her to the therapy room. She sat down on the sofa, dug noisily in her handbag, took out a cigarette and fumbled with it. A sharp scent of perfume hung over

10

her. He sat in front of her and leafed through the forms; her handwriting, scribbled and hesitant, signaled sadness and neglect.

What brings you here today? That's how he always begins his intake sessions. Fans of the cranky Viennese hold that you should sit quietly and let the client lead. But in this, he thinks, they are mistaken, or at least overzealous, as in a host of other concerns. In the night class he teaches, Introduction to the Principles of Therapy, he quarrels with them, and perhaps also with the therapeutic enterprise as a whole.

She took her time.

Somebody spiked my drink.

Someone put a drug in your drink?

She nodded: I sat down for a drink with a friend at the club. Then I got up to dance. Suddenly my head began spinning. I felt nauseous. I didn't know where I was. I started sweating. I felt I was going crazy. I couldn't breathe. I thought I was dying. I ran outside. One of the girls, a friend of mine, took me home. Since then I can't dance there anymore.

So what? he asked and immediately chided himself; too early to confront the client like this. It is useful and customary to wait, establish rapport. But his patience has been waning recently, and at any rate, those who suffer from anxiety convince themselves that

11

some disaster is approaching. This very conviction is of course their real disaster, which tortures them and destroys their lives.

She squinted: So what?

He nodded: Your drink was spiked and you can't go dancing in the club. So what?

I have to dance.

You like to dance at clubs.

I need to dance. For money. I'm a dancer at a nightclub.

A stripper.

A dancer.

He looked at her again. Dark raven eyes wide open; freckled upturned nose. Old acne scars dot her pale face. She looked at him. Here is a crucial moment, he thought. She is checking to see if I will judge or patronize her. He knew he would pass this test. He doesn't judge his clients, doesn't compete with them, and doesn't carry their load. This position is fundamental to his therapeutic approach. He is very proud of it.

Eager therapists, the people-persons who drip with goodwill and sympathy, theirs is a false promise, and theirs is a wounding touch, he will say later in class. A therapist who rushes to help forgets to listen, and therefore cannot understand, and therefore cannot see. The eager therapist, the one who's determined to offer salvation, involves himself and

12

seeks his own salvation. The good psychologist keeps his distance and does not involve himself in the results of his work. The right distance allows a deep and clear gaze. The good psychologist reserves the business of closeness for family members and beloved pets and leaves the business of salvation to religious officials and street corner eccentrics.

Such absence of involvement is not an intuitive position, he will tell his students, and is not easy to maintain. Even the cranky Viennese, who thought and spoke of it so much, failed the test of conduct, which is the ultimate test, because his curiosity and conquistador's temperament overwhelmed him. But the therapeutic enterprise itself runs counter to our basic intuitions and cannot be understood without acknowledging the value of estrangement. Why would someone spill his intimate secrets to a total stranger if there is not something healing about estrangement? Now you may say, people seek in psychologists their knowledge, not their estrangement. But those among you who are cursed with a family member who's a psychologist will attest to the futility of approaching them with your problems. A therapeutic encounter will not happen. Relief will not be found. Your relatives and friends are invested in your life. Their involvement with you is in part self-involvement, and so their view of you is distorted, which creates confusion and chafing — sparks aplenty, but neither light nor enlightenment.

The good psychologist is not infatuated with humanity, he will add later. Please, all you humanitarians rushing to the bedside, the bleeding hearts and altruists, the fragile egos among you who covet a deep tan under the light of another's gratitude, the merchants of secrets, please move over — here he will wave his hands in a dramatic gesture. (Pedagogy is theater, he likes to tell Nina, and not only in the sense that it is a deception.) The good psychologist, he'll continue, is ambivalent about people, because he knows well their treacherous nature, their potential for destruction, delusion, and deceit. The good psychologist aims to be fully present and to move correctly about the inner space. His infatuations he'd better keep to himself.

★ ★ ★

A dancer. You are here today so I can help you get back on stage?

Yes. I try to go to the club most nights. I hang around the bar. I help with this and that. But I can't dance.

And this is the first time you've experienced

14

something like this?

Something like what?

A feeling of terror and fear — nausea and disorientation that appear out of the blue, all at once.

She scratched her face and her eyes darted around the room, random and fearful like a trapped bird. Yes. No . . . umm, yes.

Who do you think spiked your drink?

Do you know who runs the strip clubs in this town?

No.

The Russian mob.

The Russian mob spiked your drink?

She fell silent.

Is there someone specific who'd want to hurt you?

Suddenly she was crying. Her eyes became red. Her shoulders shook. He waited. Finally he leaned over and handed her a tissue. He marked this moment to himself. Crying is the trail of blood that leads to the corpse in the bushes.

It's possible that we're not talking about a drug at all, he said. The experience of a panic attack is very disorienting and sudden, with no clear cause. There is a natural inclination to seek an external explanation for these feelings.

You think I'm crazy?

I don't know what that is.

You're a psychologist and you don't know what crazy is?

Crazy means insane. *Insanity* is a legal term. We don't use it.

I'm not crazy.

We are not in court.

He checked to see if she was offended by his bluntness, but she continued: I'm the featured dancer. I started a year ago and I'm already the featured dancer. My boss says that I'm the best. I make hundreds of dollars a night. But I sleep late. We'll have to meet in the afternoon.

I usually close at three.

Four is the earliest I can do.

He nodded. We could, then, meet at four.

You'll stay late for me? Her voice trembled at the edge.

I'm flexible. We're dealing with people here. Four is still reasonable.

Thanks, she said.

The treatment protocol I use is demanding and intensive. You'll need to practice, read, and work at home. We don't lie on the couch and discuss bedwetting and dreams.

I know how to work. I'm ready.

OK.

Why did this happen to me, the panic?

Everything meaningful that happens has

many reasons, never one. But that is less important now.

Less important?

You don't need to know what caused a flat tire. You just need to find the hole and patch it. You can chase a burglar out of your home even without figuring out how and why he broke in.

She looked at him, her brow furrowed with suspicion. She nodded slowly.

They got up and he opened the door. On her way out she turned and stood in front of him. Too close, he thought. Her breasts bulged under her blouse.

You can really help me?

No, he said, but I can support you in a process where you'll learn to help yourself.

He stretched out his hand. She shook it. Her palm was dry and soft.

Next Friday, four o'clock, he said, and she left.

He sat down at his desk and called Nina.

Dr. Michaels, she said.

Dr. Michaels, he replied in a softly mocking tone.

Ah, it's you. Her voice brightened.

Dr. Michaels, I need help.

Pray, she said.

To whom? God? Well, yes, as a matter of fact I had a thing with her, years ago. We were both drunk. Or at least I was. Anyway, we spent a night together. The next morning she vanished and never called back. Didn't even leave a number, and I've never seen her since. In truth, I still harbor some resentment, but I learned to forgive, to let go . . .

I can't believe they gave you a clinical license, she laughed. If your clients knew who they were involved with . . .

Who are they involved with?

Someone who hears the word *God* and relates it to sex. It's worrisome.

I also link you to sex. Isn't that worrisome?

We were not drunk, and I didn't disappear.

You disappeared.

I didn't disappear. I left.

Objectively speaking, yes, but at the level of subjective experience . . .

She fell silent.

I was in love. His voice cracked.

A short silence. Her voice softened: I will always be yours in a certain sense. You know that.

In a certain sense. Yes. Yes.

A long pause.

⋆   ⋆   ⋆

Her voice softened further: Hey, you, it's good to hear your voice. How are you doing?

OK. Busy day. A busy week.

You're taking on too much. A hypomanic episode?

Sure. You see right through me. You have a future in this business.

At least one of us has, then.

I have a new case here, a stripper with stage fright.

You're kidding.

I'm serious. Twenty-five-years old, a bit borderlinish, not entirely, neurotic without psychosis, cries easily, doe-eyed, but not empty; stands too close, anxious. Childhood trauma, if I had to guess.

Drugs?

Denies in the forms, but likely. I'll return to that later.

IQ?

Normal, it appears. Graduated high school, not that it means anything; argumentative but unpolished.

Appearance?

Outwardly directed. Not disheveled. Heavy makeup. Heels, don't ask.

Eye contact?

Comes and goes.

Attractive? Flirtatious?

Childish. Cautious.

Relationship?

Single. Beyond that I'll have to find out.

19

You are going to need my help.

I am going to need your help.

How will you pay me for my services?

You will receive respect. You will do some good in the world. That kind of stuff matters to you, if I recall correctly.

Yes. Yes, but actual compensation is also needed. I'll think about it.

Whatever you want.

I'm running to get Billie from day care. We'll talk later.

You should have married me.

You're incessant.

We were discussing you. Don't change the subject.

I have to run. I e-mailed you a picture of Billie.

Gorgeous child; resembles her mother.

Go home, you.

Home, yes. Bye.

★ ★ ★

They had met five years ago in the hospital where he used to work until he tired of the endless dead-end meetings and corridors and opened his own small office with the big name in the heart of the city. She had come for a postdoc with the hospital's Anxiety Service. One day he knocked on her door to see if he could borrow a book. She was in the middle of a phone call and motioned him in with her hand. As he was digging in the shelves, he heard her laughing and snorting; he looked up and saw her leaning back in her chair, legs crossed, a large head on a long, thin neck, short, black hair, lush lips, asymmetrical smile. Her feet, tanned, generous, attracted his attention for some reason. On her right ankle he noticed a tattoo of a small rose. In time he would caress and bite her there and she'd say, are you here to smell it or pick it?

Are you new?

Do I look new? Her eyes — curious, mischievous.

He examined her with a theatrical furrow of his brow. Used. Good condition, he said without thinking, because something in the air around her sang, and her tilted head exposed her neck, a tract of smooth, supple skin.

She laughed. If you buy me lunch, maybe I'll forget to get offended.

Lunch is on me, then.

Several weeks later, during lunch at the cafeteria in the basement, he said, we have something going on between us.

I'm married.

So what?

21

She laughed: I love my husband.

Of course, otherwise why get married? Tell me about him.

He's a carpenter by trade. But currently out of commission. He's sick. Some auto-immune curse no one can really treat or pronounce. It's complicated.

Your husband is handicapped. What chances do I have against a handicapped man?

You have no chance.

Several days later, in a crowded café at the center of town he asked, what's your most sensitive spot?

Behind the knees. That's the secret location.

He reached under the table and touched her there. Her face reddened.

Continue, she said. You're clear that we're not going to bed.

I'm not religious about this, he said. We could go to the park, to the lawn . . .

She smiled, continue.

If I were brave, or romantically inclined, I would kiss you right now.

Continue, she said.

He did. And so did she. They went on together. They rose like a river during rainy season. And when he looked in her eyes he felt as if the big bang had reversed course and collapsed back and the whole universe, the total range of consciousness, all matter and electricity had gathered at once in that dark, dense core.

Winter of that year, in a parked car on a darkened dirt road on the edge of town, they sat and listened to the calm outside.

I want to ask a big favor of you, unfairly. It's important to me that we both understand this.

Unfairness is one thing I get intuitively, he said.

I want to have a child. My husband and I have been trying for years, but with his illness and the treatments, it's complicated. The odds are not good, and time . . .

You want to have a baby with me.

I will never leave him.

I know.

Not because he is ill. Because I love him.

I know.

She turned and looked at him: Swear to me that you can contain this, that this is OK with you.

I swear.

I could never repay you. I will not try.

Nothing to repay; you in the world and happy, even if not with me, that's payment enough.

We've known each other for only a year,

maybe less, and yet I feel as if you always were . . . I trust you. And it's not based on data, but on a gut feeling. And we both know that gut feelings should not be trusted, and yet . . .

I will not betray your trust.

You think we're crazy?

We are psychologists.

Well, that explains a lot.

Not everything needs to be explained.

After that she gathered her knees to her chest, took off her panties in one swift motion, turned and climbed astride him. She led him into her with a steady hand. Her head hit the roof of the car and she laughed. She unbuttoned her blouse and leaned into him. The warmth of her skin calmed him. He hugged her. He closed his eyes and felt her on him, warm and decisive. He gathered her toward him and came in silence. They remained like this, hugging, for a long while. She took his head in her hands. She looked at him and kissed his forehead. She said, I love you. Two weeks later she collected her belongings and her books and her fingers that played magic on his skin and her husband with his cane and left. Nine months later a letter arrived, and a picture; after that an e-mail. And shortly after that the phone calls began.

The psychologist gets up from his chair and approaches the window, stretches and groans. A caravan of clients has passed through his office this day, as it does every day, leaving a blend of body odors in its wake, and the indifferent hum of the ceiling fan. At ten o'clock a new client arrived, a truck driver, wearing a stained windbreaker and a baseball cap. He sat on the sofa with the scattered heaviness of a country boy, emitted a strong scent of tobacco and sweat. A month ago he had gone deer hunting in the forest behind his house, as was his habit. As he waited silently in the bushes, his rifle at the ready, a cloud of anxiety suddenly descended, engulfed him, and chased him out of the forest. Since then, he said, he hasn't been able to sleep well. His wife is grumpy and tosses angry glances at him. Now he sits all weekend on his porch. He cleans his rifle, oils and shines it, takes it apart and reassembles it, shoulders it and points at the sky, follows a random bird through the crosshairs; but he cannot go back into the woods. Recently a biting sense of dread has snuck into his long hauls. His innards

25

twist and his breath becomes heavy every time he has to exit the freeway and take one of those narrow, winding and deserted country roads.

Hunting used to calm me down, the truck driver said. I used to go with my dad, back when he was still alive; every weekend we'd go. I used to wait all week, wait for the weekend. We used to leave at first light and sit all day in the bushes, waiting for deer. Do you know how that feels? There are days when you can sit all day and nothing shows up, maybe a rabbit, a squirrel. But that's OK. It just makes the moment stronger, when a big one suddenly appears, with thick horns. They always appear suddenly, in silence. And then you too are silent; you put it in your crosshairs, slowly. You wait for the right moment and then, boom, for one second you are God, life and death, one second here and the other over there. That's powerful.

He looked at the psychologist in exhaustion, as if worn out from the telling. He adjusted his cap absentmindedly and asked, are you a hunter?

No, the psychologist said.

The truck driver nodded and blinked, and it was clear he was not surprised by this answer.

Nothing compares to hunting, he said. You

should try it. I can sit like that all day, real peaceful. The quiet of the forest . . . You're in nature and also confronting it, if a big one appears. Hunting is in our blood. Do you know what the ancients drew on their cave walls? Hunting, hunters. We all came from there.

He scratched his cheek: And suddenly, like that, a panic attack, in the woods of all places. A panic attack, that's what the ER doc said. I thought my heart went crazy. Now I sit at home all day. Climbing the walls and getting on my wife's nerves. We fight all the time. She's not used to me being around so much. I used to be always on the road, always gone. And weekends I would spend in the forest. And she stayed at home, raised her son from her first husband, which is a whole other story . . . She would spend hours in front of the TV. Me, I can't watch much TV. After five minutes I get bored; I begin to pace around; can't stand to be cooped up. Only out in the woods I feel peace. I used to feel peace, I mean . . . until I got . . . now . . . His eyes wandered over the walls and faded.

We'll get you back in the woods, the psychologist said. You will hunt again.

The truck driver's eyes lit up.

Before he left he said, we'll go together one day. You don't know what you're missing.

After him, at eleven, another client had come in, a pudgy, middle-aged woman with thick ankles, an office manager for a lawyer in town.

I can't touch cash, she had said when they first met several months ago. Do you know how many hands come in contact with each bill? How many microbes from how many people are smeared on each bill before it gets to you? Where were all the fingers of all these people before they touched the bill that made it into your hand? This doesn't bother you? I can't just touch a bill that has rolled through so many hands when I have no idea what those hands have touched, and then touch my kids . . . Her face ashened. Just thinking about it makes me nauseous. If I were at home right now, I would go and wash my hands. I wash my hands all the time.

What will happen if you touch those bills without washing immediately?

Microbes and germs and viruses . . .

So what?

I will have to touch my children and dishes and food with these hands.

So what?

So everything will get contaminated and dirt will spread all over my house.

So what?

So . . . you could get sick. My kids will get sick.

So what?

The kids will end up in the hospital.

So what?

What do you mean, so what? My kids will get sick and they'll get, they could get infections, God forbid. You could die from things like that.

So you're saying that if you touch the bills without washing your hands, it will lead to your children's deaths?

She nodded hesitantly.

What are the odds that this will happen?

She squirmed in her chair, shrugged.

People around you, in the office, at home on the street, your friends . . . do they wash their hands as much as you?

No. I don't think so.

And their kids are alive?

Yes.

How old are your kids?

The oldest is fifteen; the younger one is ten.

You love them. You'll do anything to protect them?

Of course, anything.

Do they touch money?

Ah . . . yes. Her face was crestfallen.

If it's so dangerous, how come you let them?

Something is wrong with my head.

The fact that you recognize this means that your head is essentially fine.

She smiled hesitantly.

Your problem is more here, in your hands. He pointed at them. And the solution will have to go through your hands, too.

Since then they have progressed all the way to the exposure phase. This morning the psychologist had her again gripping a crumpled one-dollar bill and forbade her to leave for the bathroom to wash her hands. He saw her writhing in anguish and said, look at your hands, feel your disgust, experience it fully, touch the dollar bill, move it from hand to hand, squish it, press it between your palms, scrub your palms with it. Periodically he'd ask her, on a scale of one to ten, what's your anxiety level? And he'd mark it down in his notebook. After an hour and a half, exhausted and sweaty, she leaned back on the sofa, still clenching the dollar bill in her hand. The psychologist said: Here you are, holding this dollar bill, and notice how your breathing has calmed down, notice how your anxiety ratings have dropped to level two. You didn't wash and you didn't clean, and what happened? Nothing. The heavens did not open up to swallow you. Lightning didn't strike. You're still here, intact. And now you need to practice at home, once a day. Stand by the bathroom sink for at least an hour and a half, hold the dollar bill tight, let your anxiety flood you, and then you will see it recede; and whatever happens, do not wash. Record everything on this sheet and we'll continue next week.

She left, and at two o'clock the next client arrived, a purse-lipped bank teller whose tears, today as every day, began flowing even before she finished taking off her coat, sat down, and began detailing her worries. She piled them in front of him in a heap, small ones and large ones: What will happen with the car, and my husband, and the budget, and the kids? I know what's coming. It will not end well.

Those who suffer from generalized anxiety, the psychologist likes to tell his students, their dread is draped over everything and hangs on nothing in particular. If one day they wake up not anxious, they worry about this absence of worry that to them augurs some impending catastrophe. The fact that their dark prophecies fail to materialize does not lead them to abandon their worry. To the contrary, it's perceived as proof that their worry has served to forestall the disaster and prevent it, and hence they will latch onto their worrying ever stronger.

Today, the bank teller was preoccupied

with concerns over her mother-in-law, who's old already and lives alone in a second-floor apartment and who knows what could happen if she should fall one day and cannot get up or even reach the phone? She could remain like that for days, because she has no visitors anymore, which is not a coincidence, you know, since she's no saint. In years past she would badger and harass me, it's not pleasant to say but it's the truth, she was conceited, she would walk all over me, how I cook and how I dress, never a kind word. It's not easy to love that woman, believe you me. But still she is my husband's mother, and it's hard for me to see her like this. Nobody deserves this, and I'm not getting younger, either; and what about me in a few years? I know what's coming.

The psychologist returns to his chair, takes out a sheet of paper, grabs a shiny pen from the cup on his desk and scribbles absent-mindedly, trying to quell his rising disquiet. His thoughts return to the four o'clock client. What's the correct course of treatment in her case? A common anxiety protocol, he thinks, guide her in relaxation and diaphragmic breathing, teach her correct thinking habits and proceed to exposure, first here and then out there, in vivo, in the world, or in her case, on the stage. Exposure treatment for the stripper, he smiles to himself. There's poetry in everything, everything is music; just listen, and you will hear it.

His gaze wanders out the window. A mother and her daughter sit on the sidewalk bench. The mother is immersed in a lively phone conversation, and her hand chops through the air as if conducting an invisible orchestra. The girl is licking an ice cream cone. A trail of brown melting chocolate is already winding its way between her fingers. She turns the cone this way and that, studies it, contemplating a strategy. And then her tongue lunges out, a hardy battalion sent out to stop the chocolate invasion, destroy its advancing forces; but as she tilts the cone toward her face, the ice cream scoop on top tumbles suddenly and falls onto her cheek, and she, in sudden panic, angles up her shoulder and sends her tongue around to catch it. The psychologist watches her from his desk in growing disbelief. The whole scene appears to him suddenly fallacious, overwrought. This cone is too small to contain its cargo and does not at all serve the purpose for which it was supposedly designed. The psychologist wonders suddenly about the cone's cardboard dullness, and how the childish promise that you can lick around it and eat it at the end — even though it has neither smell nor taste — turns the cozy business of eating ice cream into a pressing mission, a race against time, a desperate struggle against impending meltdown, drips and stains. Desire drives people mad, he thinks. But the girl — who by now has recruited her left arm for the effort, replaced the scoop on top of the cone and pressed it onto the crumbling edges — will return years later to order ice cream in a cone, and she will circle and attack it with her tongue, and a strange giddiness will bubble up in her, as if from nowhere, as she moves to lick the trail of chocolate winding down her hand.

He returns to his papers. There is a moral element here, he intuits hazily; maybe his four o'clock is ambivalent about stripping. Maybe her refusal to dance is an expression of this ambivalence. You cannot, after all, dismiss the Viennese's contributions entirely. In some way her dancing may serve as a sort of rebellion, but so, too, possibly, her refusal to dance. And he, in his attempt to help her get back on stage, may squash some healthy voice rising inside her, a voice that seeks to pull her away from this kind of life. But who made him judge of her or her life? Are we not all ambivalent and conflicted about our work, because it is so utterly known and familiar, because we depend on it so? But is stripping a job like other jobs? Is there not an inherent dark tangle at its core? The common protocol for the treatment of anxiety disorders seems to him suddenly lacking, despite its tight logic, proven efficacy, and reasonable price. This notion of the protocol's limitations gnaws at his consciousness. To comprehend the inner landscape we must organize it; but organization contradicts that landscape's chaotic nature. The closer you get to the secret, the more of it you'll glimpse. And the more you glimpse, the less you compre-hend; the less you comprehend, the less you'll be able to see, because what we cannot comprehend we cannot see. And as your vision dims, so you'll be gradually drifting away.

The psychologist leans back in his chair, sighs, promises himself to contemplate later the meaning of his sudden exhaustion. He looks at the square gold clock that stands on the shelf across from him, a gift from Nina: *So you'll remember the time that was ours.* It's four o'clock. He gets up and walks out to the waiting room. She sits there, her legs crossed, leafing through a gossip magazine. She appears to him again at once wounded and dangerous, like a broken glass. He leads her to the therapy room.

Since that first time, at the club, have you had any other panic attacks?

She hesitates.

Well, one time, actually. I went out to the supermarket to do some shopping. I walked around with my cart. It was crowded. There were a lot of people around. Anyway, suddenly I felt dizzy, everything began to spin. The lights, the people around me, all the products on the shelves, the cans, the colors, my heart began to beat so hard, I thought everybody could hear it; everybody was looking at me. I thought I was having a heart attack right there. I felt I was fainting. I lost control, I left my cart just like that in the middle of the aisle with all the stuff in it and I ran out.

And then what?

I sat in my car. After half an hour I calmed down. I drove home.

OK, he says, you're right. This was another panic attack, like the one you had at the club. Panic attacks are a common phenomenon; very unpleasant, as you well know, but not dangerous. Nobody dies of a panic attack.

I felt I was dying. I was certain I was gone . . .

Right. This is a common sensation. But it's important to separate what is scary from what is dangerous. Not everything that is scary is dangerous, and vice versa. A panic attack is scary, but it isn't dangerous. It's like watching a scary movie, where a huge shark suddenly emerges from the deep toward a swimming girl. Everybody gets scared, but they don't run out of the theater. Why not?

Because it's a movie.

So what? Aren't they scared?

Yes, but nothing will happen to them. Or to the girl. It's not a real shark.

Right. People can enjoy a thriller because they know the difference between what is scary and what is dangerous. A panic attack is like the movie shark: you can get scared, but no need to run out. It's important to remember this. Now let's go back to your description of what happened at the store. You said you lost control.

Yes. I didn't know what was going on.

Right. That was your sensation. But our senses can deceive us. Let's say you're in a big city on a clear summer night and you look up at the sky. Will you see any stars?

Probably not.

And if you drive out of town to some dark country road in the middle of nowhere and look up, will you see the stars?

Yes.

So what happened? Are there no stars over the city?

She smiles.

Our senses do not always provide accurate information, he says. Let's look at your actual behavior. When the panic came, you left your cart; you walked out to the parking lot and walked to your car and sat there until you calmed down, right?

Yes.

Well, these are not the actions of someone who's out of control. You need very good control to leave your cart and not turn it over or run with it around the store. You need to have good control in order to find the exit door, instead of jumping through a window

38

or running aimlessly around the store. You need very good control to find your parked car, instead of wandering for hours around the parking lot or into the busy street. You need control to open the car door, to sit, and to wait. So what's the conclusion?

That I actually had control.

Yes. Despite your feelings, your behavior attests to the fact that you were in control and knew what you had to do to take care of yourself. This, too, is a characteristic of anxiety. Our senses confuse us. People who are anxious feel out of control, but they are not. It's important to understand this.

Easy for you to say. Here in your office I can understand this. But if you were there, in the store, or at the club, and these feelings suddenly tumbled over you, and your heart suddenly started beating like a jackhammer and your head exploding, we'd see how well you'd remember all this then.

Right. Exactly. That's why you'll need to practice.

Practice what?

Practice the correct way to handle your anxiety.

And how will I practice that?

This is why you're here. He gets up and drags the black leather executive chair from its place by the desk into the center of the room, right in front of her.

Sit down, please, he motions.

She does.

Now, I'll time you for two minutes as you spin around in the chair. After two minutes we will stop and you'll tell me how you feel. Ready? Go. She spins around in the chair, pushing herself with her feet. After two minutes he says, stop. She stops, breathing heavily.

On a scale of one to ten, he asks, how similar are your sensations now to what you felt during the panic attack?

Hmm, eight.

On the same scale, how scared are you right now?

Well, six, maybe, because I'm here in the office with you and I know why I'm dizzy.

OK. Here's your homework. Every day, three times per day, at home, you'll spin in a chair for two minutes. He hands her a page with a table printed on it. In this table you'll document your feelings, how your sensations resemble the panic, and how scared you are. We want to get to twos and threes, but we'll see how you progress.

She takes the sheet of paper and folds it into her purse.

That's it for now, he says, and escorts her out.

She doesn't show up for her next appointment. She does not call to cancel. There is no answer at her home or on her cell phone. She did not give him her number at work. He thinks for a while about the meaning of her disappearance. Resistance, perhaps, as the cranky Viennese would say, or maybe plain forgetfulness, since her days are busy and her mind scattered; or maybe something else, an accident, God forbid, or some emergency requiring urgent attention, or maybe this weekly hour in treatment is still a small and negligible part of her day-to-day life. Either way, he need not tangle with hypotheses. If she comes back, he'll ask her. And if she doesn't, he'll forget her. He calls and leaves a short message on her answering machine: Hi, we were scheduled for four. You didn't show up. I hope all is well. Please call if you wish to set another appointment. Take care, bye.

Introduction to the Principles of Therapy, that's the name of the course he teaches at the local college. The night class gathers twice a week in the fittingly square-jawed and severe science building. In the chemistry classroom, where faucets and sinks are fixed into the desks that line the walls, eleven tired students are splayed in their chairs. The psychologist enters with a deliberate stride. How are we doing tonight? He tosses a question into the air. The class does not perk up for him. At a glance, his practiced eyes identify in the sparse crowd the usual assortment of students who populate this type of class, at this type of hour, in this type of place: the earnest would-be therapists, the academic stragglers nearing graduation who seek to make up for lost time, the quietly bewildered. The first row, as always, is empty, except for one chair directly in front of him, where a young, glum-faced woman sits, her high forehead shining. Behind her, in the second row, sits a dipstick-thin, red-cheeked girl with bright pink hair. A few rows behind her, two young women with sparkling white

42

teeth smile broadly and politely. In the third row sits a pale student in a white button-down shirt and blue tie, busy peeling the wrapping off a bulging sandwich; in the corner two students are talking to each other. At the back, by the wall, a slumping, buff young man in a baseball cap sniffs at his coffee thermos.

The psychologist approaches the board, observes for a moment the rows of equations that were left there from the morning advanced chemistry class, mumbles, did we get this? and proceeds to erase vigorously. Then he turns back toward them and looks on. It's the third week of the semester and he still does not recognize them by their names and faces. All young people, to tell the truth, look similar and distant to him, like the members of a strange and exotic tribe. Their names and their faces tumble around in his brain. He has learned over the years how to read a name from his class roster and raise his head slowly, catching the brightening face of the student whose name was called and turning nonchalantly toward them. This trick works well with new students, but those who have taken his classes more than once are aware of his method and smile under their breath in bemusement.

He steps forward and stands before them.

43

Subtle delight courses through him. They are in his hands, like soft clay. But his delight is not because of that, but because he knows that his hands are good. With the passing years he has gradually freed himself from the burdens of youth. No longer does he court their favor; no longer does he seek their admiration or acceptance. No longer must he prove his command of the material. The material has become a part of him. He is the material. He doesn't fear them and doesn't need them, and therefore he is relaxed, and his comfort emanates from him and floats about the room like an invisible cloud, and they inhale it and relax as well.

The good psychologist deals with story and identity, he announces. And he who deals with story and identity deals with memory. All your events and experiences, all your insights and history, all that is bound and wrapped into your notion of *I* — it all depends on memory. That's why it is important to know something about memory processes. Most people know nothing about memory, and if they have any idea, then it is usually wrong. Your own understanding of memory, we may therefore assume, is faulty, and our job is to correct it. He waves his chalk in front of them. I am going to write a number on the board, he says. I will leave it on for a few seconds and then I will erase it. Any one of you who manages to forget this number will earn an automatic A in this course. They perk up with palpable suspicion. He writes and immediately erases:

64381976217

Now he turns toward them and says, forget, forget now, forget with all your might.

They laugh, and the slacker in the back row says, forget what?

Memory. Now there's a tricky business, the psychologist says as he paces in front of them; but before we demonstrate that, let's first understand that *memory* is a verb, not a noun. It's a process, not an entity. It's a journey, not a destination. A person does not have a good memory. A person may be good at remembering.

The psychologist stops and stands and looks at them.

Some of memory's tricks are no doubt familiar to you. On one hand, there are things that you would like to forget but cannot. Take, for example, the name of some useless celebrity — as opposed to, of course, a useful celebrity — that you wish to forget; to clear, perhaps, some room in your brain for more useful information, even though this idea, too, is based on an error to which we will return. Anyway, for our purposes now — he looks over at the brawny, baseball-capped, sleepy kid in the back row, who's leaning back in his chair against the wall — Steve, please give us an example of someone like that.

The sleepy kid tilts forward and lands the front legs of his chair gently back on the floor, looks this way and that, and says, my name is Eric.

Eric, of course. Give us an example, if you will.

Example of what?

Of a useless celebrity.

Ahh, hmm, the pope?

The pope, fine. Let's suppose you decide to erase the memory of the pope from your brain, to clear some room in there for the principles of psychoanalytic theory, which we covered last week and on which you will be tested next week; will you be able to?

Able to do what?

Erase the pope from your memory.

The brawny boy shrugs his shoulders: No?

Right. You will take the memory of the pope to your grave; to your grave, and perhaps even beyond that, if we take the pope's own word on this. You, Eric, will carry the memory of the pope with you forever.

And beyond that, the whole idea that your memory is like a library where more and more books are stacked on long shelves until there's no more room — that notion too is wrong; popular among university students, to be sure, but wrong nonetheless. Your memory is not a library. In fact, the more you know, the easier it is to remember more. But we will return to all this later. Now let's see who among you has managed to forget the number I put on the board earlier.

Cautious smiles awake around the room.

Show of hands, he says.

Their hands rise slowly, except for Jennifer's — or is it Janet or maybe Jessica? — the stone-faced brunette at his feet who is shattered by even a hint of failure and who attempts, against the spirit of the moment but in keeping with her deep nature, to remember exactly.

I believe you, he says, smiling. You all believe that you have forgotten that number. But unfortunately for us, for you, it turns out that whether we can retrieve a memory depends in part on how we inquire about it. So, for our purposes, let's phrase my question differently, in the form of a multiple choice item.

The number I asked you to forget was:

a. 2
b. 0.5
c. 30
d. 64381976217.

Now the room creaks and moans. Eric smiles to himself and returns to his nap; Jennifer clenches her teeth and considers the whole demonstration a tasteless, even malevolent exercise. The kid in the tie in the third row sits upright, his face sealed as always, his hands at rest in his lap.

Your grade, the psychologist says, you will have to honestly earn with your hard work and dedication. But here we have the first lesson about the nature of memory: what you wish to forget, you may not be able to. What seems to have died, perhaps is just asleep. On the other hand, sometimes you wish to remember something, and there it stands at the doorway of your consciousness and refuses to come in. You know you know something, the name of some useless celebrity, perhaps, and yet you cannot fish that name out of your inner aquarium. And this illustrates a critical feature of memory, which resembles, as it turns out, most of the processes in the internal realm: the same cause will regularly yield different, even opposite effects.

Notice if you will: in the external, physical

world, an act may have linear and predictable results. If we shine a bright light in your eyes, you will go blind. If we hit you over the head, you will faint. If we light the flame under the kettle, the water will boil and then evaporate. The internal realm, on the other hand, is guided by different rules. Take the issue of trauma. At times, the details of a traumatic event are erased or obscured, either because clear remembering threatens the integrity of the self, as was the argument of Shlomo the Holy from Vienna, or because stress interferes with cognitive processes in general, as Yerkes and Dodson have demonstrated. But sometimes the exact opposite will occur and the memory of a traumatic event, in all its elaborate detail, will grab hold of the brain like a nasty weed that cannot be uprooted. What would the sufferers of such a fate not give to forget their pain, the source of their pain? But for naught.

Jennifer — he turns to the tense brunette in front of him — perhaps you have an example.

An example of what? She stiffens in her chair.

An example of some painful issue in your life, a troubling issue that you are willing to share with us, a painful thing that's grabbing at your mind that you wish to forget.

Ahh . . . well, I'm engaged, and we're

planning a spring wedding, and there's so much to think about. The dress, the reception hall, the band, the guests, the seating arrangements. The food. And I'm taking dance lessons, and I'm also on a diet, to look good in the dress that I haven't picked yet, and the flower arrangements and expenses, the budget . . . I would like to forget all of it, and the hairdo, everything is so expensive . . . Her voice trails off.

The psychologist smiles at her warmly: Indeed, a conundrum, in a well-known sense, but there is hope, because this too shall pass; as the poet Robert Frost said, life will go on. And only a great poet can begin a sentence with the word *life* without disgracing himself entirely. But let's get back to our business. He straightens up. What was our business?

You asked for a painful memory, Jennifer says.

He nods. Yes, but try to remember something from your distant past. He looks around him. His eyes meet with those of the boy in the tie in the third row. He gestures toward him.

Me, I have so many painful memories — seems like my whole past is a painful memory, the boy in the tie says somewhat hesitantly. You see, until recently, I was lost and completely confused. But everything is different now; everything has changed since I found my way, since I trusted my life over to Him . . .

Well, it looks like you've found a path that is right for you, the psychologist says.

This path is open for everyone, the boy in the tie says, his voice growing confident; and right for everyone.

Perhaps, the psychologist says, but this every person must decide for themselves, as you have done, and I'm still looking for a memory . . .

I had a cat, Eric pipes up suddenly. His name was Meow, and he fell into a well and died. I was six years old. I actually cried.

The psychologist nods, good example. You'd rather forget Meow's bitter end, but you cannot. The cat, and the pope, of course, will remain in your memory to the grave.

You really know how to offer comfort and encouragement, Professor.

I am describing the processes of memory.

A faded smile flickers across Eric's face, and it appears he's reassessing rather unfavorably his decision to wake up.

Here's the sum of my wisdom about cats, the psychologist says, and an indulgent chuckle rises from the class to meet him: Whoever you are, your cat always lives better than you.

Jennifer leans forward to write in her notebook.

My cat is dead, Eric mumbles to himself glumly.

You, the psychologist says, looking over the room, may believe that memory is but a video recording that is documenting the days of your lives as they happen and storing them in the brain's archives. This is a common assumption and an intuitive metaphor, not lacking in elegance: the brain is a library in which the tales of our times are bound and housed; a beautiful metaphor, but, alas, erroneous and misleading. Memory is not a storage place but a story we tell ourselves in retrospect. As such, it is made of storytelling materials: embroidery and forgery, perplexity and urgency, revelation and darkness. He steps forward with practiced theatricality.

Take a piece of paper, if you will, and write on it my whole lecture so far, verbatim, word for word.

Jennifer leans forward and begins to write feverishly. Eric hesitates, scratches the back of his thick neck, adjusts his cap, and stares into space with his poodle eyes.

Let me save you the trouble, the psychologist says. None of you are going to pass this test, because your memory chews up and digests the raw materials that are, in this case, my words. It does not swallow them whole. You can remember what I was talking about.

But you cannot remember what I said. What was I talking about, Eric?

Ahh . . . the pope, and my cat Meow, and about things we want to forget but cannot remember.

The four o'clock client sits on the blue sofa. She grips a large, square handbag, yellow with black dots, and then lifts and turns it over and spills its contents onto the seat cushion. She searches the pile impatiently, pulls out a cigarette, rolls it between her fingers, and then stuffs it back into the bag. She leans over and gathers the piled contents with her bent arm, shoves everything back inside, and wrestles to close the bag. She puts the handbag on her knees, and then beside her on the sofa, and then on the floor. Her gaze pauses over his for a split second, and her face seems to him suddenly murky.

We had an appointment scheduled for last week, the psychologist says. You did not show up.

I forgot.

You forgot.

Yes.

Are you generally forgetful?

No.

So . . .

I forgot. I'm sorry.

The psychologist looks at her and nods.

Such forgetfulness requires attention, he thinks, as it denotes in all likelihood some ambivalence about the therapeutic process. On the other hand, sometimes a cigar is just a cigar, as the cranky Viennese famously said, and even a matter that requires attention is not necessarily an urgent matter. He mulls it over in his mind and finally decides to return to the protocol.

In our last meeting I gave you some homework . . .

I don't have time for practice, she blurts impatiently.

He hesitates. Perhaps she's testing him, exploring the limits of his compassion. Perhaps she has known rejection and rushes to dismiss preemptively, before she is dismissed.

You don't have time to help yourself heal?

I do, but not for exercises.

He nods. Resistance, as expected. And here a sudden urge gathers within him. Cut and let her run, he thinks. Send her home. Those who do not wish to work should not show up for work. Both of us could save precious time, and is there any other kind of time? Please return when the need to contend and confront ripens. But he says: Tell me three things that you did for yourself this past week. Not for money, or for someone else, but for you.

She ponders in silence.

I touch myself, she says, raising her eyes to look at him.

A provocation, he thinks, as would be expected. She opens with her most familiar gambit. His gaze rests on her face, businesslike and half-empty.

You masturbate, he says.

I touch myself.

You masturbate. It's important to call things by their proper name.

She nods. Her gaze drops. She rubs her skinny fingers together.

That's one thing. I asked for three.

Silence.

I bought a new handbag, she says finally and points. And these. She lifts the handbag to her lap, opens it and pulls out a pair of round sunglasses with gold rims. Nice?

That's two, the psychologist says.

She sighs: I went out of town yesterday afternoon, just for a drive.

Yes.

I like to drive out of town. Just to drive around in the country. If the weather is nice, I put the top down. Then you can see everything around you. It relaxes me, the wind, the colors . . . I especially like animals.

Animals.

Horses, sheep. But I like cows the most. Cows.

She nods, her hands in her lap, her gaze lowered.

Tell me more.

I always loved cows. I grew up on a farm, you know, before we moved to the city. I used to milk them. Did you ever notice how every cow has its own moo? A personal moo. It makes me . . . Do you think I'm crazy?

I think you are a keen, sensitive observer.

The cow's shape, it appeals to me: skinny legs and a thick body, very modern, clean. Like this handbag, only without the yellow. Most people don't see these things, but I have a fashion sense. I have aesthetics. And cows like to stand. They hardly ever move. You'll rarely see a cow going crazy, out of control. They are peaceful. They stand in the field and eat, and once in a while, there's this moo . . . I think about it a lot. In India, you know, the cow is sacred. It gives milk; it's a mother; it's life. And inside this square body there are many stomachs, a complicated system. My dad told me that. Four stomachs, maybe five? Many stomachs. We would ride by feedlots in his truck and see the beef cattle and he would say, look, steak, steak! He would laugh about it . . . She chokes up slightly. There are places, you know, like India, where you can't touch them. And here we slaughter them without thinking twice. But I'm a vegetarian. And here to be called a cow is considered an insult. A cow. All they see is the fat, the meat.

She pauses for a moment. Then she proceeds: The cow, for me, has strength. And helplessness, too. The cow has no self-defense. It's completely exposed. No speed, no claws or teeth, no poison, no wings. It can't climb a tree. It can't dive under water. It can't fly. Only moo, moo . . . Her voice evaporates into a whisper: moo, moo.

The psychologist watches her silently. Here it is, after all, hidden behind the heavy makeup and the invisible internal scars, among the weeds of her deserted inner garden — a life, humming, observing. There's an engine under the hood, rusted, perhaps, out of tune, coughing and leaking from long years of neglect and yet an engine exists, horsepower, not just hollow space, not a mere defeated carcass. His heart stirs toward her. He leans forward. You grew up in the country, he says, right? Well, fears are like mice in the fields. Nobody likes mice, but if you run away from them, if you deny their existence, they will only multiply and ruin the crops and gardens, take over the house. You must go after them and hunt them down. The same is true with fears. You are training here to become an anxiety hunter. Not an anxiety victim. Not anxiety prey.

Anxiety hunter, she mumbles.

An anxiety hunter. And you cannot learn to become an efficient hunter without going hunting. Nobody learns how to hunt by talking.

He gestures with his hand toward the black executive chair. She nods.

We'll continue next week, he says, and he gets up to show her out.

After he walks her out, the psychologist returns to his office. He leans back in his chair and looks out the window over the sidewalk. Two giggling girls float by on their way to the coffee shop around the corner. One has black hair and wide hips, and the other is close-cropped with a boyish gait. His gaze trails after them, and for a moment their lightness sweeps him up too. He gets up and pulls out the file of his four o'clock from the desk drawer. He leafs through it. Then he grabs his clipboard and looks over his session notes. He likes to hold the clipboard in his lap and write short comments and quotes during each session. But now he realizes that he did not write anything during their session except the words *masturbation, shopping, cows*. He calls Nina to tell her.

You will probably see some poetry there,

she says wryly, but have you thought of maybe ending this habit of yours? If this is what you're scribbling there, then really, what's the use? And beyond that, the clipboard in your lap creates a distance and connotes formality. It's a physical barrier between you and the client. This is not good.

The barrier exists anyway, he says. The clipboard gives it a proper material presence, and it's better when abstract things acquire a symbolic physical expression. It's easier on people.

It's easier on you, she says.

Those borderline clients who cut themselves, he says, do so to localize their amorphous pain. Notice, if someone dies at sea and we can't find the body, we still search after it persistently, as if it matters. Why does it matter? The body rots either way. I'll tell you why: the body and the grave are realizations of an abstract notion. They symbolize a feeling. This is where the pain resides. This is where it collects.

How did we get from your clipboard to the grave of a dead sailor? she laughs.

My clipboard is a monument to distance; it captures it, and the client remains free to deal with closeness. Besides, you know we cannot trust memory alone. We must document. I for one have a memory of you in a field at night, on the warm hood of a car, the sweet taste of your nipples. Did it or did it not happen?

A memory like that you really should not rely on, she laughs.

I don't rely on it; I count on it.

OK, you, focus for a second now. Next month I'm at a conference in Chicago. Schacter is giving a talk, speaking of memory. Aren't you interested?

Chicago. Love that town. Are you coming with the family?

I will be on my own.

Schacter fascinates me. I'm a big fan of Schacter.

Go home.

Bye.

He puts down the phone, laces his fingers behind his neck, stretches back in his chair and closes his eyes. Faint joyous music ascends in his mind, lilting, tremulous. A door has opened. He is going to see her again. Soon. Her face, face-to-face. And these words dance blithely in his head: her face, face-to-face; her face.

The psychologist leaves his campus office and shuffles on his way to the science building. The chilled evening air swipes and caresses his face by turns. He cups his palms to his mouth and blows into them to warm them up, but to no avail. A chill spreads through his body. He turns abruptly and enters the library building. In the lobby a new coffee shop has opened recently, donated by one of the city's wealthy residents, an alum who graduated eons ago with a degree in literature and history and has since made a fortune in the used car business. The psychologist walks to the counter, looks up at the menu that is etched on the earth-colored wall.

Coffee, he says, black. The girl behind the counter squints at him and points eventually to a table in the back. There he picks up the heavy thermos, pours himself a cup, pays and leaves. He hugs the cup in his hands, and its warmth, spreading through his fingers, feels like a small miracle of mercy. A strange giddiness overcomes him. When he enters the classroom he notices Jennifer glancing at her watch and furrowing her brow.

Am I late? he asks.

She nods.

I am not late, he says. The professor, as we know, is never late. The professor is delayed. Students are late.

She purses her lips. Behind her, two sets of white teeth smile brightly.

He stands in front of them, drinks carefully from his cup, its warmth fading, and asks, how are we doing tonight?

A lethargic groan flickers from among the chairs and subsides.

He turns to Jennifer and says: Jennifer will tell us now what is new and different in her life. What did you do this weekend, Jennifer, to take care of your soul, to uplift your spirit?

She looks at him with surprise and suspicion, as if examining an unfamiliar food item. I studied for the test, she says finally; I read two chapters ahead.

She seems haggard and wilted to him suddenly, and he feels a stirring of compassion. He steps toward her and leans gently over her: What did you do for your soul, your heart — he hits his chest with his fist — for pleasure, just to have fun? What did you do this weekend to enjoy life?

She slumps into her chair. I enjoy reading ahead, I enjoy getting prepared, she says.

He nods in acceptance and retreats slowly,

raising his eyes to the window.

An unexamined life is not worth living, so said Socrates. An unlived life is not worth examining, so said I.

Jennifer leans to take notes. In the back row, Eric's face produces a faint smile, but it's unclear whether he's responding to the events around him or to his own thoughts.

Last week we discussed memory, the psychologist says. We learned how memory is a reconstructed story concerning past events and not a photograph or a copy of them. Today we will look into memory's schematic nature. I am guessing you all have heard the saying, *seeing is believing*. And it's true. But the opposite is also true: *believing is seeing*. Our brain does not process events only mechanically, based on our internal circuits and wiring alone, but also subjectively. Perception is a dance, joining together the external properties of things with the properties of our perceptual mechanisms and with each person's own life experience. Memory processes, their nature and their limitations, along with our expectations and habits — they all interact in shaping what is remembered.

He sips from his cooling coffee cup and approaches his computer. An overhead slide appears on the screen behind him.

He points at the slide, waits a few seconds and says: You all see something. Most of you probably read, *I love Paris in the springtime*. But look again.

A hushed moan of recognition rolls through the classroom. Eric leans forward, his mouth agape and his head shaking from side to side. His foggy expression morphs into a silent plea.

Focus, the psychologist says. Read every word separately.

The boy's face creases and then lights up.

Our brain makes shortcuts, the psychologist says. Because of prior knowledge and habit you were expecting to see a grammatically correct sentence, and so you skipped over the actual sentence in front of you, the actual sensory input. We do the same when we remember. Let me read to you a list of words. Try to remember them in order without writing anything down. Jennifer sighs in frustration and sits up. He reads slowly and deliberately:

night	dark	relax	pajamas
blanket	breathing	sheets	rest
pillow	dream	slumber	repose
bed	snore	lie	quiet

Now, he tells them, to distract you for a while, I'll tell you a story that I read in the paper not long ago. A Dutch TV station decided to break a record in the *Guinness Book of World Records* and arrange a row of four million dominoes. More than a hundred people worked on the project for weeks in a large suburban airplane hangar. One night a lost bird flew in through a window that was left open by mistake and in its frenzy and fright knocked down twenty thousand dominoes. Luckily, the workers had left spaces here and there in the domino chain, and therefore not all the dominoes fell. The frightened bird huddled in a corner of the hangar, and an expert bird hunter was called in and shot it with a BB gun. The following day it was discovered that the bird belonged to a rare, endangered species. Wildlife organizations began calling for the hunter to be tried in court since Dutch law permits killing endangered species only if they pose a risk to public safety or crops. The hunter received death threats at home, and a competing TV station announced a prize for anyone who would break into the hangar and finish the bird's job by toppling all the dominoes. He stops and looks around.

And what happened then? Jennifer asks.

That's not the real question, he says. The real question is, what is this story about? And to that we shall return later. But now let's get back to our memory business. I will now write three words on the board. By show of hands, we will decide which of these words appeared on the list I just read:

Sleep
Bed
Eucalyptus

Who remembers *sleep*?

All hands shoot up, except Jennifer's; she looks around her hesitantly, raises her hand halfway, and then folds it back in her lap.

Bed?

All hands rise.

Eucalyptus? They laugh. Eric raises his hand with a sardonic smile.

Good, the psychologist says. Here I have, without any difficulty, implanted in your minds — the finest minds in the land, mind you — a false memory. The word *sleep* was not on the list at all. The memory of the word *sleep* was made up by you. And it is no coincidence, of course. It did not happen because there's something wrong with your mind, but to the contrary, it happened because your memory is normal and as such schematic, not literal, and therefore given to bias and distortion and failure. So, what can we conclude? Eric?

Ahh, I'm not sure. But your list made me tired all of a sudden.

Yes, the psychologist says, yes, I'm tired too. What may we conclude, Jennifer?

That we can't count on our memory?

Right, he says. A psychologist who relies on his memory alone engages in hubris and self-deception; popular preoccupations in our time, to be sure, but exhausting and barren nonetheless.

The four o'clock client sits in front of him on the sofa, leans forward and scratches her ankles. Her hair is pulled back; she is wearing tight, dark jeans and a black blouse with a plunging neckline. She rummages through her bag and pulls out a crumpled sheet of paper.

Here's your homework, she says.

Yours, he says, your homework. He looks over the paper. I see progress. What did you learn from this exercise?

That your treatment is not like the shrinks in the movies.

What did you learn about anxiety?

That feeling nauseous and queasy is not the end of the world. Just don't tell me I have to go through this for another week.

No. He turns to his desk, opens a drawer, takes out a small, round mirror and hands it to her. Take this mirror, hold it in front of your face and stare at your reflection. Two minutes, go. He watches her. She sits upright, serious, holds the mirror to her face. When two minutes are up he says, the sensations you've just felt, on a scale of one to ten, how much do they resemble the panic feelings?

Six or seven, she says. I felt a little like I was floating outside of myself. Like everything is unreal. That's weird how it happens from looking at a mirror. You got tricks, Doctor.

What's the level of fear?

Five, maybe, not really fear. Weird.

OK. He takes a clean sheet of paper from his desk and hands it to her: Three times a day, two minutes in front of this mirror. Don't move your eyes. Try not to blink. Record everything.

She stuffs the paper into her bag.

I'm interested in what you get out of stripping, beyond the money, the psychologist says.

I don't know, she says.

I have a rule here, he says. You cannot say *I don't know* about yourself. Your actions and thoughts are yours, they emerge out of you, and you always know something important about them. And if you don't, then guess. Your guess doesn't arise from the air, either, but from within you. It too is a sort of knowing.

She plays with her fingers.

Power, she says finally.

Power.

She nods: All eyes desire.

The fact that all eyes are on you, desiring you, gives you a sense of power?

Not exactly me.

Then whom?

Her.

Who's she?

I don't know.

He stares at her intently.

Your rules are annoying, she says with a faint smile.

He waits.

You're the great psychologist. You're the expert. You explain.

She's testing him. Here he should wait and let her reveal herself in the telling, or in the failure thereof, fans of the Viennese will admonish; but something in him cracks open, and a subterranean calculus swirls in his brain.

She's someone who feels weak, he says.

She nods.

She feels lonely, neglected, hurt.

She nods again.

She's a child.

Tears. A single tear, actually — thin, humble — slips quietly down the valley between the hill of the cheek and the ridge of the nose. And it is not accompanied by a squinting of the face but travels by itself, alone.

The psychologist leans back, takes the box of tissues from the desk and hands it to her. She pulls one out, blows her nose into it weakly, and then kneads it in her hands that meet between her thighs.

Tell me more about her, she says.

In a sense she's like all girls, he says in thoughtful deliberation. She plays with dolls. She dances in front of the mirror. She day-dreams. She loves candy. But in another sense she's different.

How is she different?

She has secrets.

Every girl has secrets.

She has scary secrets.

You're wrong, she says. She doesn't like to dance in front of the mirror.

She covers herself up in a blanket, he says. She's in a warm, protected cave.

No. She hides at night in the closet.

She hides, he repeats.

She nods.

He looks at the clock. The hour is over.

Our time for today is up, we'll stop for now, the psychologist says. We've made progress.

Your rules are annoying.

The rules are mine, and the annoyance is yours, and it's allowed here, even welcomed. Thank you.

Thank me? For what?

For your emotional expression. Your frustration is a human emotion. It's evidence that you are one of us.

One of us?

A human being. Not an extraterrestrial. Not subhuman. Not half-human. Fully human, with all the attendant emotions. That's good.

You're weird, Doctor.

What makes you say that?

You say thank you when I get angry.

What did you expect me to say?

The people I know don't say thank you when I get mad.

Maybe they are weird.

The next day, in his office on campus, he buys a ticket to Chicago on the Internet. In the conference program, he notes Schacter's lecture, On the Sins of Memory, seven of them, no less. Through his window he looks at the manicured lawn, framed by angled lines of trimmed bushes. An endless procession of young women in low-cut jeans passes by on the path between the library and the campus center. He no longer covets them but their essence, the scent of youth that emanates from their supple, shining skin. Amid the cacophony of clothes in all colors, the blouses, the shawls, the chains and the hats, still a piece of naked skin always attracts his attention, like a distant oasis. What is the secret of naked skin? he wonders to himself. How is it that among all these textures and colors and cuts and layers and sheets of cotton, Lycra, satin and silk, a patch of naked skin alone sings, alone beats like an infant's heart among the piled blankets, resonates in such vivid singularity? Does it all go back to Harlow's poor monkeys, clinging fiercely to their cloth mother? Suddenly he can feel his heart pounding. How long since he last saw Nina? Four, five years? He remembers their last night, before she left. She snuck out of her house with some excuse and came to his apartment. They sat at the square table and he made tea.

All packed? he asked.

She nodded: The movers are coming tomorrow morning. So many boxes . . . unbelievable. Until you move, you have no idea how much stuff you've been hoarding.

You, you've been hoarding.

Yes, me.

Then she took his hand in hers. They sat like that, face-to-face, bent silently over their teacups. After that he walked her to the door. They stood at the door, and then he kneeled down, put his hands around her waist and leaned his head on her stomach. She held his head tight.

I will wait for a sign from you, he said.

Even before she left he made a promise to himself to leave her be completely, as he had vowed to her. He made a law for himself to keep his distance, not to go visit, even though she's only a six-hour drive away. Not to interfere or dig for information. To jive and flirt, yes; to chat and talk shop; but about the child he would not inquire, and he would never pressure or plead. He would let go, and he would move on.

* ★ ★

He calls her.

Dr. Michaels.

Dr. Michaels, he returns, smiling.

She cracks her burned laughter: It's you again.

Is there anyone else?

Someone like you, no.

Is that a put-down or a compliment?

Both.

Ah, that old ambivalence.

You did not call me so I could slap you around. What's up?

I bought a ticket to Chicago. Where will you be?

At the Hilton. I arrive on Friday.

I'm coming in Friday evening.

Good.

I'll meet you at the tiki bar downstairs, in the corner under the plastic coconut tree across from the wooden hula dancer.

You spend much time at the Hilton? she asks.

There was a conference last year. After two lectures I had to escape. You know how that goes. Two academics in a room immediately suck out all the oxygen. One says *paradigm*, and the other says *qualitative data analysis*. Any sane person will be overcome by suicidal impulses and seek to run away . . .

To the tiki bar?

I wouldn't settle for anything less than refined, you know that.

OK. It's set.

If you wear the strapless black dress, the drinks are on me.

We're not going to bed.

So, will the bed come to us?

Stop it. I'm in a fragile place with my husband. His situation is deteriorating.

I see.

And you will not try anything.

I'll try everything.

You will not succeed.

The process is important, regardless of the outcome, just ask Schacter.

Go home, you.

Tonight we will discuss a common confusion among young therapists, he announces to the class: mental health — to the extent that there is such a thing as *mental* and such a thing as *health* — is not a destination but a process. It's about how you drive, not where you're going. The therapist is like a driving instructor, not a chauffeur.

In the second row in front of him, the girl with the bright pink hair giggles and leans forward to whisper something in Jennifer's ear.

He turns toward the pair: As I said at the beginning of this class, everything that's uttered here is the intellectual property of the whole class. So you will now tell us, kindly, what's so funny.

The pink-haired girl casts a guilty look in his direction. You've got funny examples for everything, she says finally.

The psychologist nods. This is the fundamental principle, he says, here in the classroom and there in the therapy room: without an example to illustrate your point, you have no point.

Can you illustrate this point? Eric asks.

The psychologist smiles and continues: Therapy is foremost an act of language. Language by its nature is symbolic. The word *tree*, for example, neither looks nor sounds like a tree. And language is metaphorical. If Eric tells his girlfriend, I gave my heart to you, and you broke it . . .

Those are some old-school lines, Professor, Eric says. My game is more contemporary, you know?

Of course it is, but work with me, the psychologist says. Such a line is literally nonsensical. You didn't actually give her your heart, and she didn't physically break it. And yet your girlfriend is neither confused nor critical. She knows exactly what you mean, and is quite taken with your surprising old-school eloquence. Language is symbolic and metaphorical, and so the meaning of any one word, any one object, emerges from its connections to other words and objects. A lone object, like a lone word, like a lone ant, has neither prospects nor import. We comprehend something only in terms of its ties to other things that are like or unlike it. The right metaphor can reveal hidden meanings, blast tunnels through mountains of confusion, lure the truth out of its cave. And metaphors are all around you, should you care to see them.

He stops and points at Eric: Throw me a topic, anything.

Ahh, cars, Eric mumbles, sitting up slowly.

The psychologist smiles: A used car acts in ways that may contradict the owner's manual. The gasoline gauge, for example, may be stuck on *empty* regardless of how much gas is actually in the tank. The car's owner, if he knows his car's eccentricities, will not panic at the sight of the gasoline gauge and will not rely on it. The client who shows up at your office is a used car. If you help him understand the idiosyncrasies of his inner gauges, he will know how to interpret them correctly.

Sports, Eric says, give me one about sports.

Sometimes life seems like a game of tug-of-war. You feel pulled by superior forces and your first instinct is to plant your heels in the ground and pull back harder. But maybe it's more useful to let go of the rope. And . . . the psychologist can coach, but only the client can play. And the coach will never score a goal, a basket, or a run no matter how much he yells and sweats and jumps around. And in mental health, as in sports, even the best must practice daily.

Bikes! says Eric, now fully awake and buzzing, I live for my bikes. The pink-haired girl turns and looks at him.

Sometimes our balance depends on movement, the psychologist says. A forward momentum, regardless of the direction of movement, is at times a stabilizing force.

That's the bomb! Eric rejoices. What about the ocean, the beach? he sparks.

Think of a swimmer trapped by an undertow. His response would usually be to try to swim against it. But that would cause him to tire, cramp, and drown, done in not by the current, mind you, but by his erroneous response. To save himself, the swimmer should let the current carry him to sea, where it will dissipate, and the swimmer can paddle around and back to safety. The same principle holds true for our negative emotions, which should be accepted, even though the impulse to push against them is strong. And overall it is important to flow, to release, not to cling to the past, not to cling to a diagnosis, or to the common protocol; to let go, like I did here in this lecture that was supposed to focus on the process of mental health but ended up examining metaphors. The therapeutic territory is often a disaster area, prone to earthquakes and floods. In that environment, those who cling to yesterday's terms blind themselves today and lose tomorrow. Someone who collects many possessions is in a certain sense defined by them, and will cling to them when the flood arrives and will perish with them. He who lets go, who gives up his stuff and seeks a higher ground, will live to collect another day.

I won't cling to anything, except my bike, Eric announces victoriously, and my bike will take me to a higher ground.

The pink-haired girl lowers her head and giggles softly to herself.

Have a pleasant flight, the flight attendant says, but there are no pleasant flights. There are only more or less tolerable flights. The flight to Chicago is less tolerable. The flight attendant reminds him to buckle his seat belt. Like all flight attendants on short regional flights, she is sour and does not smile, as if she had been banished unjustly from her rightful place on a more lucrative transatlantic flight. In case of an emergency landing, she lectures through the creaky speakers, the seat cushion can be used as a flotation device. In case of a loss of cabin pressure, oxygen masks will drop from the ceiling. If you are traveling with a child, put the mask over your face first and then put on your child's mask. The psychologist contemplates her monologue, the deep strangeness of this repeated recitation of the details of a future catastrophe, at once explicable and inconceivable. How many flight attendants on how many flights have plodded laconically through this same speech, which every passenger has already heard-but-not-heard a thousand times; heard but did not internalize; heard but suppressed; heard and derided; heard and shuddered? And has any passenger on any doomed plane ever been saved by this flotation device, saved by hugging the filthy pillow with all his insignificant might while the giant metal capsule spirals down in smoke through the clouds and into the ocean, that sleepy and efficient mortician? A waste of words, he thinks to himself. Why go on plugging this sad and hollow speech to no end? The oxygen mask issue, on the other hand, appeals to him and brightens his mind considerably. The mother should put the mask on herself before putting on her child's mask. Seemingly, this move contradicts the basic intuitions, but in fact, he thinks, it illustrates nicely the principles of healthy altruism. He could make good use of this analogy with his clients. Not the indigent ones, who may never have been on a plane. And he must be careful since any mention of a plane tends to increase the heart rate of his client base in general. But the well-fed urbanites, the petite bourgeoisie forever fretting over their failure to find comfort amid all their comforts — they could click with this analogy: care for the other begins with self-care. And while he's busy contemplating this matter the plane has descended and landed.

As he exits the terminal a cold gust of wind greets him abruptly. He huddles inside his worn leather jacket, raises his shoulders, buries his head between them and curses at the air. A yellow cab appears and the driver, a balding man, heavyset and dark skinned, walks toward him with a noticeable limp and asks in a foreign accent, where to?

Hilton, the Loop.

The driver takes his bag and tosses it into the trunk, closes it with a thud and slips back into his seat in one practiced motion. They get sucked into the stream, and the driver settles immediately into a phone conversation that appears to have begun years, or generations, ago. The phone is hanging on his chest, and a small earpiece is shoved in his ear. He waves his hand and speaks excitedly in an unfamiliar, grating and throaty language. Then he bursts into hearty laughter. Then there's a short silence. The driver turns to the psychologist, angles his eyes to the rearview mirror in the universal cab driver move.

First time in Chicago?

No. I visit periodically.

Business or pleasure?

Business, he nods politely.

What kind of business?

Psychology.

Treat people?

Yes, and I also teach.

I don't believe in psychology, the driver says.

You're not alone. What do you believe in?

Allah.

You're not alone.

My daughter wants to study psychology.

She doesn't believe in Allah?

The driver shrugs: She doesn't know. The city confuses the young people.

Confusion is no crime.

If you have Allah, you don't need confusion.

The driver stops under the brightly lit canopy at the hotel's entrance. Two doormen in pressed uniforms approach them.

Hilton, the driver says. He steps out and takes the bag from the trunk, puts it on the ground, stuffs the money that's handed to him into his coat pocket, slips again into his seat and sticks his head out the window: Do you have children?

The psychologist hesitates; a stinging current charges through him.

No, he says, and immediately regrets it, and immediately forgives himself.

The driver manages a sorrowful nod: With Allah's help, you will. He turns away and disappears in the ceaseless stream.

The psychologist walks into the lobby. The reception clerk, who seems too young, plucks at his computer keyboard with curt efficiency. Within minutes the psychologist is in the elevator, on his way, through the carpeted corridors, to room 314. He walks in, tosses his bag onto the bed, enters the bathroom, checks himself in the mirror, runs his hand through his hair, and goes down to the tiki bar. A waitress in a miniskirt, who also seems too young, greets him with a bright smile. He nods at her and scans the room, and before his eyes can adjust to the darkness he hears Nina's voice.

Hey, you.

Her figure materializes from the darkness.

Hey, he says, Dr. Michaels.

They hug. He holds her tight, and for a moment he can feel her entire body against his, the softness of her breasts through her silk blouse, the warmth of her stomach, the scent of her skin. Her hug is cautious, not surrendering, and within a second she looks to pull back gently.

Wow, she giggles after he lets go.

He smiles: Who do I have to appease to get some alcohol in this dive?

Only me, she says. Don't strain, you'll pull a muscle.

They sit at a square corner table by the wooden hula dancer.

When did you get in?

About an hour ago.

Ahead of me.

What's new? She waves over a waitress and orders a vodka tonic.

Brandy for me, the psychologist says.

So you're taking the brandy route? Nina says.

The high road, he nods. He looks at her. Her skin glows in the dim light. Almond-shaped eyes, the crooked curve of the lips. Her hair is short and severe, as he remembers it. Her neck is elongated; thin, broad shoulders.

Tell me how you're doing.

Overall OK. I got a job offer from Palo Alto. The Center for Behavioral Medicine. They are willing to double my salary.

Far away from here, he mumbles.

Yes.

You will leave academia?

I'm a clinician. I like old, burned-out, broken down and disabled people. Young shining students spoil my mood.

You will move to California? What will your husband do?

We'll buy an old house. He'll work on it.

How is he doing?

Up and down; unpredictable day-to-day. Right now it's deteriorating somewhat. He's dizzy and has vision problems, difficulties walking. A month ago he collapsed on the stairs.

The psychologist nods.

I hope he gets better, he says.

She sends a steady, darkened gaze at him.

A part of me does, he says.

She nods slowly. Her expression softens.

How is it between you two? he asks.

She sighs. OK. We communicate. Moving to the city will be good for him, I think. Being close to his family and to a decent medical center . . .

The psychologist reaches into his coat pocket, pulls out a crumpled plastic bag and from it a small teddy bear with cymbals in its hands. For Billie, he says. Tell her it's from you.

You're sweet. She leans over to kiss his cheek.

The waitress materializes and hovers over them with a tray of drinks. She puts two glasses on the table. As she leans down he sees the contours of her breasts through the generous opening of her blouse. They appear to him like heavy udders, and a sudden delight ascends in him at the sight of their yielding ripeness.

There will be another round, he tells her. She smiles and nods.

How are you? Nina leans forward.

I did not get any job offers. I see clients. I teach a night class.

You have someone?

No. I'm working. I'm an aging melancholic. I'm not going anywhere. I'm damaged goods.

Women love that.

I don't meet women. I meet university girls and anxious clients.

You're avoiding, you're closing up.

I am interested in only one woman, he says.

Lucky woman, that one, she smiles.

Perhaps, he says, perhaps. Either way, these are the facts. He drinks from his glass. The bitter liquid burrows through his body, warming him up. He leans toward her, looks at her intently, reads tenderness and whimsy in her eyes.

She looks at him. Something is bothering you, she says.

One more brandy and it shall pass.

It won't pass; it will just be forgotten for a moment.

I want to sleep with you.

I can't right now. I told you on the phone.

So let me look.

Look?

You can lie naked on your bed and I will just look at you for five minutes, and then I will go to my room and go to sleep. I promise.

No hands. Just to see once more your inner thighs, your nipples.

She tilts her head. I can't, but please continue.

Sometimes a flash of memory shoots through me; in the middle of the day, the image of your nipples as if from nowhere. My knees buckle midlecture. I wonder what Schacter would have to say about this. I remember touching them for the first time, that summer by the fountain across from the optometry department. There was a squirrel in the bushes, you got frightened and they popped up.

She laughs: Poor squirrel, taking the blame like this.

Every good memory should include a squirrel in the bushes, he says.

And breasts, on the woman's side at least, she says.

And a fountain, on the man's side, he says.

And an optometry department, she says.

Well, maybe that isn't necessary.

She smiles at him warmly. You look well. I missed you.

Same here, he says. And here we are and I still miss you.

After this they remain at the table for a long time. He drinks too much. Finally she says: I'm taking you to your room and you're going to bed. What's your room number?

314. Yours?

I'm 328.

Close. I'll come by and knock on your door tonight. I won't be able to sleep.

You will not come. You're drunk. You're going to bed.

And if I come, will you open?

No.

You will.

I won't.

You won't forget to give Billie the teddy bear?

I won't.

There's a button in the back that turns on the cymbals.

Let's go up.

She helps him up from the table, holds his elbow, and twines her arm with his. They leave the bar and head toward the elevator. The hostess at the door smiles farewell. Inside the elevator they stand hugging. They exit the elevator and walk down the hall in a slow coordinated stride. The soft carpet swallows the sound of their steps. All is quiet.

I hate hotels, he says. A hotel room is like a hooker who changed her panties for you.

Thanks for coming, she whispers.

You thought I'd miss a lecture by Schacter?

No, of course not, she smiles.

They arrive at his door. He takes the key card from his pocket.

Good night, she says. She leans in and kisses his cheek. She stands in front of him, takes his hand and puts it on her breast. He closes his eyes. They stand in silence. She removes his hand, kisses the back of it gently, lets go, turns around and walks away. His aching eyes trail behind her. He wants to chase after her, to grab and hold her, but he concedes. He enters his room, crawls between the velvety sheets. Before he falls asleep the image of his four o'clock client materializes suddenly in his mind. In her high heels and red lipstick, she's hiding scrunched up in her childhood closet, her eyes wide open.

At 4:10 the four o'clock client storms in, shakes raindrops off her coat and sighs heavily. She spills the contents of her handbag on the sofa and rummages through them, takes out a lighter and a crumpled cigarette.

You can't smoke here, the psychologist says.

She looks at him resentfully, thinks it over, and resigns herself. Your rules, she says.

Annoying, he nods.

A half smile blossoms on her lips and shrivels: You said you would help me.

I said you would help yourself. You disappeared for two weeks, again.

I got depressed. I sat at home.

I called. You did not answer.

I didn't answer the phone.

Right.

He waits quietly.

She settles into the sofa and looks around restlessly: Who selected these pictures here?

He shrugs: Me.

A female touch is missing.

You seem troubled.

My boss is all over me. He wants me to get

94

back to work. Get on stage. I explained to him that I have a problem, that I'm in therapy. But he, he doesn't care about these things. Hooligan. I have one month to get back on the stage or he's going to throw me out, he says. Can you help me in one month?

No, but you can help yourself.

Yes, yes. Clichés. I pay you $150 an hour to help myself?

Right. I will do my part. Your part is your responsibility. Everyone has to piss for themselves.

She lobs an alarmed look in his direction, as if stung by his directness. Yes, she mumbles, you and your examples. Annoying. She looks around her in pronounced impatience. OK, what now?

You will need to show up for every appointment, on time. You will need to do your homework.

She purses her lips.

Silence.

You don't have to go back to stripping, he says finally.

What do you mean?

It's possible that your stage fright is an expression of a healthy and authentic need, of some ambivalence you feel about your

95

current life, your work. A voice inside you is calling you to stop.

She scratches her cheek. I have a voice inside me that wants to stop living. Should I listen to that too?

Yes, he says. It's important to get to know the inner conversation. Listening does not mean agreeing or choosing sides, and it does not compel you to act. Listening means an acceptance of reality, in full, and that's important.

I make five hundred dollars a night dancing. If I left the club and worked as a cashier in some convenience store, I would not be able to pay you.

He waits.

I pay my rent, she says, I bought a car. I'm saving money for tuition. I have a plan. I'm going to buy a house, get a lawyer, and get custody of my girl. I'll —

A girl? He cuts her off. Did you say a girl?

She looks at him, hesitates. Then she nods. I have a little girl.

You have a little girl. He sits up, jots notes on his pad. He waits.

She's with my ex. He beat me. I left him. He has money. He took her.

Took her? How do you mean?

His family is in my hometown. They're powerful. His mother the witch has a big

96

restaurant there. He's like her baby, an only child. She gives him everything. He's had it easy. He used to buy me dresses, clothes, shoes. He bought me a bike. I didn't know anything. She helped him scam me.

Your ex's mother . . .

Yes. She got a lawyer. I was then . . . I was in bad shape.

What do you mean in bad shape?

I got caught with cocaine, OK? She hardens suddenly; a tweak of anger registers on her face. The bastard brought it home and then he tattled on me behind my back. I'm sure his mom the witch arranged it. She knows everyone there. The police eat at her place every day. She knew we were fighting. The bastard probably ran to her to tell her I threatened to walk away with the baby. I was pregnant. What he didn't tell her of course was how he was pushing me around, shoving me, and more than once. This asshole would come home from work drunk, and I would tell him to get off me, let me rest. And he's like come here, come here, do this for me, feed me, cook for me, blow me.

Do you see your daughter?

Once a month, usually.

How is she?

A good kid, but she loves him more. She told me she loves him more because he gives her stuff. He's got money.

You didn't tell me you had a daughter.

What's that got to do with my problem? I need you to help me to get back on stage.

What's her name?

Michelle.

Michelle. You didn't mention her.

I didn't come to get help for her.

Everything is linked, he says. It's a central issue in your life that you didn't bring up.

You didn't ask.

You didn't note it in the forms.

You write everything in forms?

I wonder why you decided to omit this detail.

I need to watch out.

Watch out?

Yes. It's complicated enough already. Do I know who you report to? I don't need more obstacles in my way while I'm trying to get her back. I have a plan.

He sits quietly and looks at her, knows that she's wrestling with herself, yielding slowly. Let the client come to you. Never work harder than the client. He waits, like a parent whose child swore at him in a fit of rage and is now looking for a way to reconcile. And he suddenly hears in his head the sound of a child's sweet laughter, swirling inside him like an autumn leaf; a clear and distilled laughter.

She covers her face with her hands. He leans forward and says, tell me about Michelle.

Yesterday I asked her to help me in the kitchen and she said she couldn't because she had plans. I said, what plans? And she said, I have plans but I didn't plan them yet.

She laughs softly and he nods.

This evening he drives to the recreational center for his weekly basketball game. For years they have been gathering there, a group of aging men, for two sweaty hours of chasing a bouncing ball. On his way there he thinks about this ritual, which is on its face so insignificant. And yet he is surprised every time anew at how these games so readily lift his spirits. On the court he greets the usual gang with high fives and scattered chatter. He knows them well by their court personae. Here is the permanently put-upon guy, forever seeking a reason to explode in indignation; there's the guy who must win at all costs. Here's the timid man, who always thinks pass. And still he knows nothing about them. They are opaque to him beyond the walls of this court. They have never gone out drinking together. He has never visited any of them at home. He ponders for a moment whether the others do meet out there in the world; whether he's been left out of the circle — due to some intuition, a reaction on their part to the subtle air of detachment emanating from him, or because he does not have a wife or children. He ponders this but decides it isn't so.

When he returns home he showers, and then he calls Nina. Perhaps she's in her office late tonight, he thinks, but there's no answer. He sits at the computer and writes her an e-mail: *Thanks for the night in Chicago. It was good to see you again. Suddenly hula girls get me going. Anyone who dismisses Pavlov is an idiot. How time flies . . .*

His hands are steady on the keyboard but his words suddenly gush out from a different place: *Where are your fingers your dulcet lips your inner thighs the scent of your secret your shadowy whispers the darkened valley at the small of your back the bars of your rib cage come over come over.* He pushes back from the desk. Breathe, he says to himself, breathe naturally; your emotions spilled over. Accept it, let it go. You are human. Your feelings are like weather in the world. Where are your feet right now?

His mouth is suddenly dry and he gets up and walks toward the kitchen. As he passes through the darkened hallway he senses a faint presence at his back, as if a child is walking behind him. An invisible child is walking behind him, widening her steps to place her tiny feet in the footprints that are pressed in the carpet. The psychologist ambles silently through the living room. He does not look back. The image fills him with delight and alarm. The unseen child follows in silence.

His four o'clock client sits erect on the sofa, her legs crossed, her hands clasped at her knees. I had a dream, she says. It means something, doesn't it?

Does it mean something to you?

She fumbles with her fingers. Her pupils widen.

I dreamed voices, she says.

Voices.

In my dream there were voices, echoes. Nothing to see, and I wasn't anywhere. Not light, not darkness, just voices.

What did you feel?

Warm feeling, like when you take a bath. Nice.

What did the voices say?

Nothing, they were voices, but they weren't talking.

Human voices?

I think so. Pleasant.

He nods: What do you think this means?

You're the doctor. She reaches for her bag, pulls a cigarette out, fiddles with it, and stuffs it back in.

Unembodied dream, he says quietly.

Unembodied?

Voices with no form. You canceled the body in the dream.

Maybe I want to die. The body, you know what they say, it's just temporary storage. Full of pain. Falling apart. The soul is eternal . . .

I don't know about that, the psychologist says, but let's focus on the notion of *maybe I want to die*. That's a problematic statement.

Talking about death scares people, particularly doctors, she says.

The problem is not with the content but with the structure.

Perhaps you want to explain in plain English.

It's not accurate to say, *I want to die*, because in a sentence like that the word *I* echoes in the brain as *all of me*. And it's obvious that not all of you wants to die. It's better to say, *a part of me wants to die*.

Mumbo-jumbo. What's the difference?

Try it out. Say, *a part of me wants to die*.

A part of me wants to die.

Yes, and then there's another part. What does it want?

To get back my daughter.

Good. Now you have clarified for yourself the situation as it is.

She is silent.

Reality has many layers, he says. And it

pays to observe them from different perspectives, to get a fuller, more accurate picture. In your head, in all our heads, a conversation goes on, with many voices participating. It is important to listen to all of them. The loudest voice, the one that shouts and pushes and shoves, is not always the smartest one, or the right one. To say *I* is to use a crude generalization. Sometimes it works, a useful shortcut; but usually, or at least when it comes to important issues, you'll do well to listen up close, give the shy one, the stutterer, a turn at the microphone.

She nods.

Let's practice, he says. Tell me about an event in your life that brought up emotions.

She stares at him.

Silence.

Pregnant silence.

Sometimes I wake up at night and I see on the wall a kind of hazy stain moving, slithering around, she finally says. Like a grayish octopus. Sometimes at night I feel like I hear steps on the carpet. And someone walks around my room, and sometimes it's like someone sits on the edge of my bed. I feel the edge of the mattress sinking.

And what do you feel at these moments?

Scared.

A part of you feels fear, and another part?

Curious.

And what does the curious part have that the fearful part does not?

Courage?

Yes. And this courage is also yours. Fear is an important consultant, but a lousy leader. You can listen to its advice, but you must not let it lead. Courage is a wise leader. You should follow it.

Tonight we will begin with two anecdotes, he announces to the class, two pearls of therapy lore I fished out for you from the depths of the archives. And here's the first: one day a young child with a bedwetting problem arrived for treatment at the office of the famed psychiatrist Milton Erickson. Erickson did not mention bedwetting at all and did not turn to hypnosis. He learned that the boy was a baseball fan and spent the whole hour describing in detail to the child the coordination that is needed to catch a baseball in flight. The mitt must open and close at precisely the right moment, and similarly, when you prepare to execute a throw, you must release the ball from your grip not too early or too late, but at precisely the right time. When the session was over the child went home and the bedwetting stopped. And here's the second story: another canonical psychiatrist, Theodore Reich, was talking to a patient who told him she had just visited the dentist, where she received an injection and her tooth was pulled. As she was speaking, she suddenly pointed to a book on the shelf in front of her and remarked that it was upside down. Reich said, why have you not told me you have had an abortion?

The psychologist stops and waits and looks around him. Eric, it seems, is napping as usual under his cap. Jennifer leans over her notepad, writing feverishly. The white teeth girls sit with their mouths agape. The boy in the tie in the third row caresses his tie distractedly.

What is the point? the psychologist asks. What do these anecdotes signify?

Hush in the classroom.

Two insightful therapists, Jennifer says finally.

My father is like that, Eric says. He can tell you what's wrong with your engine without even looking under the hood. He just looks at your car driving and he knows immediately what's wrong.

The boy in the tie raises his hand. The psychologist turns and nods to him.

First, I would say, the boy begins tentatively, these two therapists have the spark of the divine in them. What you described are moments of grace. Also, I want to be clear that I am against abortion, and I hope that the Lord's mercy and compassion will penetrate this client's heart and return her to faith.

The boy in the tie falls silent and puts his hands in his lap. Eric, behind him, sighs and rolls his eyes.

The psychologist nods: Moments of grace, no doubt; but those anecdotes also exemplify, for our purpose, a common approach to the therapeutic process. This approach, which I will term *the big bang theory*, holds that a successful treatment is characterized by a movement toward the killer insight, the miraculous climax, the rattling catharsis that will release dammed-up emotions, clarify obscure meaning, teach the deep lesson, wash away the pain, unearth what was buried and rotting like a dead body, and a new dawn will bathe in light what was previously dark and opaque, ushering in a new inner order, peaceful, coherent, rich and intact. The big bang theory offers an enticing, seductive vision; an elegant narrative for therapist and client alike. What therapist does not yearn to be the agent of such a definitive transformation? Who does not wish to untie the obdurate knot with one pull of the string? The client too connects with this idea, identifies it easily within other realms of life, from sex to a nice bowel movement through court dramas on TV, where the brilliant lawyer pulls out the ultimate question, or a forgotten piece of evidence that tears instantly through the villain's web of lies. For this conceit too we may blame Herr Sigmund, who, in his messianic zeal, stamped this narrative into the therapeutic ethos and beyond, into popular imagination, so that it is now taken for granted.

He stops and raises his hand.

The big bang story is iconic. It's the dream of the handsome prince who kisses Sleeping Beauty and takes her to a life of wealth and happiness. It's the dream of winning the lottery. But waiting for a dreamy prince is not a serious relationship strategy. And the hope of winning the lottery is not a serious plan on which to base your financial future. And the story of therapy, here, in this world, is different entirely. This you must remember and accept: there is no purifying insight. There is no magic wand. There is no big bang, only small tremors, each meaningless on its own, like subatomic particles that have no mass of their own but create it through their motion in space. And even if there is catharsis, still the true healing occurs afterward, after the kiss, after the waking up, after the insight and metaphor, and it is embodied in the gray repetitive grind of daily practice, of learning a new language, stuttering, with clenched teeth.

Let's focus on your thinking style, he tells the four o'clock client. Our thoughts translate external events into internal meaning. If the translation is awkward or distorted, then we get confusion and error. Thoughts are like viruses. We all learn the importance of physical hygiene in protecting our bodies. You know it is important to wash your hands, cover your mouth when you cough, brush your teeth. But no one teaches you mental hygiene. The problem is that an incorrect thought, if it enters your mind, is like a virus that has entered your blood. It can cause pain, suffering, and death. Suppose you are at home by yourself in bed on a winter night and suddenly you hear a loud thud outside your window. That's an event. How will you react? Well, that will depend on what you tell yourself about the noise. If you tell yourself, it's just snow falling from the roof, then you will turn and fall back to sleep untroubled. But if you think, there's a burglar at my window, trying to break in, then fear and panic will set in, and you'll reach for the phone, or for your gun. Let's take a specific

111

example from your own life. Two weeks ago you showed up here feeling down, because . . .

My daughter said she loves her father more than me.

Right. But that was not the reason for your foul mood. The reason for your mood was your interpretation of your daughter's statement, the meaning you decided to attach to it. Let's track your internal monologue. When the girl said what she said, what did you think?

That she doesn't love me; that I'm losing her, that I'm a bad mother.

OK. Now look at these interpretations. These are thoughts, and thoughts are not facts; they are guesses, hypotheses. And hypotheses must be tested before they are embraced as truth. Perhaps it is possible to interpret what your daughter said differently.

Like how?

Like, that children change their minds minute to minute. Doesn't she ever cry and scream like the world is ending, and then she sees some chocolate and suddenly she's all smiles? Or you may think she's testing you. Maybe she feels not entirely loved and reflects it back to you. Maybe she's trying to stick it to you a bit because she's angry about the separation. Maybe she's just rambling, or repeating something she overheard. Maybe you didn't hear her right. Maybe you've heard other things, opposite things that you have chosen to forget. Maybe it's an opportunity here for you to explain to her that you are not mad . . .

OK, I get it, don't get carried away.

Apologies.

That's OK, she smiles.

The thoughts you settle on will determine how you will feel and what you will do. That's why it is important to shop around before buying.

Shop around?

Yes. I want you to regard the process of choosing your thoughts like you regard the process of choosing a new pair of shoes. You like shoes, don't you?

You've noticed.

Yes. When you enter a shoe store, do you buy the first pair you see?

No.

Right. What's first is not necessarily what's best. Same thing with your thoughts. The first thought that comes to your mind is just that, first. It is not necessarily the right one for you. So, how do you decide which shoes to buy?

I walk around the store and compare.

You compare, based on what?

The brand, the size, the fit, the style, the price.

Correct. You look for evidence, information that helps you decide consciously which shoe is the best for you.

Yes.

You must use the same method to choose your thoughts. Your brain is a thought store. Every time you feel anxious or down, the feeling stems from a thought that you have bought. An ill-fitting thought, like an ill-fitting shoe, will hurt you. That's why you need to monitor your thoughts, your interpretation of events.

You want me to think about my own thoughts?

Exactly.

That's hard . . .

Living like you do now, in fear and suffering, is also hard. The choice in this life is not between easy and hard, but between kinds of hardship, between a hardship that gives birth to wisdom, compassion and mercy, and the hardship that keeps on replicating itself to no end.

I thought you psychologists were in the business of promoting positive thinking.

We are in the business of promoting accurate thinking. Your thinking habits are like your posture habits. If you sit in front of the computer for hours with a hunched back, at some point you will begin to feel a backache. To get rid of it, you will have to learn to sit up straight, with good posture. Incorrect thinking habits cause mental pain and therefore need to be changed. Accurate thinking is a habit you can develop, but only through daily practice.

She straightens up in the sofa unwittingly.

Sometimes, the psychologist says, certain habits that may have worked before cease to work as time and place change. Think, for example, about a boy who grows up with an abusive parent. Every time this boy tries to express himself, to speak his mind, the parent slaps him and ridicules him and tells him to shut up. If the kid is smart, what will he learn?

She's taken aback slightly. He watches her, wonders if he's ventured too close to her wound, but she purses her lips, holds back tears, and says, he'll learn to shut up.

Yes, that's the behavior, but what are the thoughts that cause it?

My opinion isn't important. Speaking my mind is dangerous.

Right, and after a few years of that, this thought becomes automatic, like language. And let's suppose the child grows up, leaves home and goes to college. He's at a different place and time, but he carries his habits with him. So, he's sitting in class, and the professor turns to him and asks him a question. What thought will come up first for him?

Don't talk. Danger.

And what will he do?

He'll stay quiet. He'll say, I don't know.

Right, and this behavior, the one that used to save him from getting beaten up at home, is now working against him. The teacher isn't happy; the other students think he's not serious. What should he do?

Speak up. Speak his mind.

And what kinds of thoughts will lead to this?

My opinion matters. Speaking up here is OK. It is not dangerous here.

Right. This thought, which is accurate, given the evidence and current circumstance, he must accept and use repeatedly, say it to himself in his head, and act from it, until it becomes automatic, a new, healthy habit, like tying your shoelaces, like language.

★ ★ ★

After she leaves he documents the session in her file: *The client is working, motivated, good cooperation. Began working on cognitive restructuring, the principles of accurate thinking.* Before he leaves he approaches his desk, leans over and sees that a new e-mail has arrived, from Nina. He sits down to read it.

I had a good time as well. Sorry I couldn't give more. And (maybe) that I couldn't drink more. Attached is a picture of Billie with her new teddy bear. His name from now on is Teddy, which means we have given up on the originality award, but the beauty award, as you'll see in the picture, we're winning hands down. Take care of yourself (up close) and of your stripper (from a proper distance). Yours, Nina.

His eyes linger over these last two words. He rolls them on his tongue, takes in their sweetness, their tartness. He thinks about writing back right there, but a worthy reply does not formulate in him. He gives up, turns off his computer, locks his office, gathers himself into his car and drives home.

Those of you who are still awake, please close your eyes for a moment, the psychologist says to his class. He scans the room. They obey, all except Jennifer, whose suspiciousness won't let her yield. He writes on the board:

Don't Read This Sentence

OK, open your eyes, he says. They look at him, and he gestures toward the board. Eric sighs dismissingly and Jennifer bends to write in her notepad.

Even if you wish to comply, to do as you're told, you will not be able to. Why is that?

The class is quiet. A chair squeaks.

Because we know . . . , pipes up the pink-haired girl.

Know what?

English? she mumbles.

Yes. And this knowledge imprisons you. You cannot escape it. What you know you cannot unknow. That's why knowledge is dangerous. Learning will redefine your world, irreversibly. Watch this. He walks to the computer.

A line of single digits shows up on the screen behind him:

$$8 - 5 - 9 - 1 - 7 - 2 - ?$$

He points at it: These digits are organized by a hidden sequential logic; if you discover it, then you'll know what the last, missing number might be.

They hunch over their notebooks, scribbling, calculating; scratching their heads.

After a few minutes he stops them and says: The right answer, which I bet none of you has, is zero. The last number should be zero.

What's the logic? Jennifer asks, clearly perturbed at her apparent failure to crack the code.

The logic, he says, is that this is not a numbers problem.

What problem is it, then? Jennifer asks.

It's a word problem, he says. They look at him suspiciously.

A word problem? the pink-haired girl chirps.

He nods: If you spell out the name of each letter, you will quickly see that they progress in alphabetical order: **E**ight, **F**ive, **N**ine, **O**ne, **S**even, **T**wo . . . And the only number that starts with a letter after T is **Z**ero, of course.

119

Of course, mumbles Jennifer.

He waits a long moment, studying their faces. Do you see? They nod.

Tricky, Eric mumbles in appreciation.

What was until just now, to you, a math problem, and as such impenetrable, has turned into something else entirely: a phonetic problem, and as such not much of a problem at all. How did that happen?

You told us to think about the names of the numbers, not the numbers themselves, the pink-haired girl says.

Right. New knowledge has changed your approach, your path, and your understanding. You now see with new eyes. And there's no turning back. For good or ill, once you know, you cannot unknow.

Jennifer looks alarmed.

He turns to her: You and your fiancé, if you'll allow me a blunt example . . . (She nods and slumps down a bit into her chair.) Suppose you return home from class one evening and find him in bed with your sister. You will have learned something new. Now you could forgive him, you could leave him, you could join them in bed . . .

Eric wakes up and nods with enthusiasm.

The decision is yours, the psychologist continues, and it's not for me to judge, but either way your understanding of your reality, of your fiancé, and of yourself, has been altered significantly — irreversibly.

The boy in the tie squirms in his chair with apparent unease, strokes his tie with his left hand and raises the other.

You may not judge them, he says. But I'll remind you that there is a judge. There is a judge whom nothing can evade.

The psychologist smiles faintly. Perhaps, he says, but we cannot know for sure. And even if there is a judge, it remains unknowable whether it is the judge you believe in or one of the other notable candidates. What we can know for certain is that Jennifer's reality has changed.

My fiancé would never do that, Jennifer mumbles, and I don't have a sister.

No, of course not, the psychologist sighs, I didn't mean it like that, I was speaking metaphorically. An unpleasant sensation swirls and grips inside him and he commands himself to breathe and let go. His gaze glides out the window.

You came here to study, to learn. You were told from an early age that learning is important, that it is important to expand your mind; that education will make you wealthier and make your lives richer; and all this is true. But it is not the whole truth. Knowledge is a double-edged sword. That is why we are ambivalent about knowledge. That is why you and your future clients will not always wish to know everything, not that it is possible to know everything; which reminds me of a story about an ancient ruler who summoned his wisest adviser and asked him, what does the world stand on? The world, said the wise man, stands on the back of an elephant. What does the elephant stand on? asked the ruler. The elephant, it is known, stands on the back of a turtle. What does the turtle stand on? The wise man tugged at his beard: The turtle stands on the back of another turtle. And what does this turtle stand on? Another turtle. And that one? The wise man threw his arms up in desperation: I promise you, sir, it's turtles all the way down. But where were we?

Knowledge is a double-edged sword, Jennifer says dutifully.

Thanks, Jennifer, he says. And this is not the end of our troubles because above knowledge, at least in the evolutionary sense, hangs another such sword — awareness.

What's the difference? the pink-haired girl asks.

Well, awareness is the knowledge of knowledge. Think if you will of a zebra in the African savanna. It doesn't walk around thinking: I'm a bad zebra. What kind of zebra am I? What will I do with my zebra life? Why not?

It can't read? the pink-haired girl asks with hesitation.

Yes. It does not have language, and sophisticated thinking requires language. That's one reason. What else?

It's not self-aware, Jennifer says.

Elaborate, please.

It doesn't know it exists.

Indeed, the psychologist says. Human beings have evolved two systems beyond the zebra: the ability to represent concrete reality using symbols, mostly through language, and the ability to know something about knowledge itself. What, you may ask, is the relevance here? What does the zebra have to do with therapy? Well, the zebra knows how to do many things: to find food, to escape a predator, to mate and raise its young. But it is not aware of its knowledge — so far as we know. We are not granted the zebra's simple existence. We, as human beings, must navigate the realm of self-awareness, and that is not easy. For example, all of you have been sitting in front of me and blinking periodically. You know how to blink. But now that you are aware of your blinking, your blinking has changed. You are thinking about it: Is my blinking normal? Can others see my blinking? Will I ever get rid of this forced blinking? Awareness burdens knowledge with all manner of distraction. The same is true for our linguistic representation. The zebra has a lion to contend with. And the lion is sometimes present and sometimes gone. We have the lion but also the word *lion*. And the word is always present, always accessible, even after the real lion has vanished. There's a story about two monks, an old master and his young eager apprentice, who meet a young woman by the river. The water is raging, the woman says, can you carry me over? The old monk lifts her up in his arms, takes her over, puts her down on the other side, and the monks continue their silent march. After a few hours, the apprentice can no longer contain his turmoil and alarm. He turns to his teacher and says: How could you take that girl in your arms? Don't you know that such contact violates our laws? I, says the old teacher, left the girl by the river. You are still carrying her with you.

He looks around the still classroom and waits.

What does this have to do with us? he asks.
The zebra, Jennifer says, sitting up, doesn't think about the lion when it's not there. But we can think and talk, so we take the lion with us everywhere! And we make connections, we develop associations — like what we

learned about Pavlov. It's like the word *lion* meshes in our heads with the real lion until the word by itself makes us just as scared as the real thing.

Yes, the psychologist nods, he leans and smiles at her. That's why we get no rest. Ghosts haunt us, sometimes all the way to the psychologist's office. That's why the psychologist's work is to teach the client to separate the words, which are crude generalizations and labels in the mind, from concrete events and things in the world. Sometimes a word may become so overloaded with heavy meaning that it paralyzes and tortures the client. Such a word needs to be neutralized, emptied a bit. The word *lion*, after all, has no teeth. And the label *anxiety* is but a slogan, a rather makeshift summary of a nuanced and delicate human experience. When the client says, *I'm anxious*, we must recognize that his situation is not *an anxious person* but *a person who's aware of his anxiety* or *a person who says he's anxious*. The awareness and the labeling are more problematic than the bodily sensations they claim to represent.

I don't get it, Jennifer says, her forehead creased. You say that humans are designed for awareness; we are not zebras. And then you say that awareness ruins things and causes us problems. If these problems are inevitable, a necessary result of our design, then what is therapy for? You cannot turn us into zebras, can you?

Correct question, he says. And the answer has two parts. First, awareness is not only a hindrance. Second, the zebra part is alive in us still. Regarding awareness, it is also a bridge. The part that observes the object by definition must be outside of it. Fish don't know they are in an ocean. That's why when the client says, *I'm sad*, it is important to clarify to him that such a statement is inaccurate. A part of him is sad. That is the truth. The sad part experiences sadness; it knows sadness. But he also has another part of him that exists outside the sadness and is aware of it. The aware part knows *about* sadness, and is therefore able to dialogue with it, to manipulate it. In crisis, such awareness allows us to leap backward and forward in time and space, which enables us to keep proper perspective. If I'm depressed, my awareness enables me to see the boundaries of my depression, which are not visible from inside it. Hence I can glimpse my depression's end; hence I can have hope.

At the same time, the zebra's ability to live fully in the present moment, to go with the flow of being, has not been completely rooted out of us. All of you have at some point felt a

126

moment like this, a peak experience, in Maslow's words. Try to recall such a moment, when time opened up and stood still; when you felt at one with the universe and the living moment in unforced control, boundless joy; when you were deeply, effortlessly awake, bathed in awe and wonder. Surely you can remember a moment like that?

Orgasm, Eric announces from his place by the wall. The pink-haired girl shudders slightly. Jennifer frowns. The psychologist waits.

Prayer, the boy in the tie says suddenly, when you feel the presence of the Lord in your soul.

A week ago I was washing dishes one afternoon in my apartment, Jennifer mumbles. I hate it when the sink is full of dirty dishes. Anyway, suddenly I saw an albino squirrel through the window. It stood in the middle of the lawn. Its tail was twitching left and right, like it was undecided what to do. It was holding a big nut in its paws, twirling it all around. It was looking around. Suddenly it ran and jumped up the tree and disappeared. And I noticed that five minutes had gone by. Water was filling the sink. Suddenly I realized I had just frozen that whole time, with my towel in my hand; I didn't notice anything around me. I was sad when it was gone. And I don't even like squirrels; they always seem to me like rats with fancy tails. Her voice cracks. Does that count?

It counts, says the psychologist quietly, and he notices that the class has quieted down too, as if holding its collective breath. This moment of yours, and the telling of it, these are the tools of navigating the internal space. Knowing the moment and knowing about the moment.

The psychologist sits in his chair and tries to gather his rambling thoughts, to quiet his mind and focus on his four o'clock client, who sits on the sofa, her legs crossed. The truck driver showed up this morning feeling up. Two weeks on the road without any panic, he said. The breathing exercises are helping. I'm ready for the next stage, Doctor, ready to go out into the woods, hunt some anxiety, like you say. The office manager, in her turn, told him that her fear of touching cash has lessened some, and with it the frequency of hand washing; but instead, new problems are emerging. She finds herself arranging the coat hangers in her bedroom closet, checking and rechecking the gaps between them, and she's arranging and rearranging the cans in the kitchen cabinet, making sure all the labels point forward. The bank teller, through the curtain of her tears, said her constant worries were worrying her, and continued to list various bodily discomforts and vague ailments in detail: stomach pains, nervousness and lack of sleep. Her muscles ache. She cannot concentrate. And what if we run out of money? What if I'm suddenly bedridden, or if I'm fired? Maybe I'm making mistakes at work. If I write one digit out of place it could ruin the life of a customer, and paperwork is endless there, and I always have to recheck my work and count the change again and my boss complains that I'm too slow, which only stresses me more ... The psychologist listened patiently, and at one point, as he listened, a thought snuck up inside him of a possible encounter between the office manager and the bank teller, on both sides of the counter, this one gingerly touching the dollar bills and the other nervously recounting the change. He toyed with the image in his mind for a second but then recoiled, sensing a certain disgrace, dropped it into the river of forgetting and returned to focus on the bank teller ... and I also stress my kids. They go out and I force them to call me all the time and they don't understand what's wrong. And my husband also complains that I nag him, and I worry that he'll run out of patience with me and leave me, and then what? I know what's coming.

★   ★   ★

Where did we leave off last week? the psychologist asks his four o'clock client.

We spoke of thoughts, how to buy the right thought, like a good pair of shoes. She stretches her long legs forward. I bought a new pair, by the way. You like?

We spoke of Michelle, he says, about your reaction to her saying she loved her father more.

Yes.

We said it was important to shop around before buying, not to hurry to buy negative thoughts.

Yes, she says, staring at her shiny shoes.

And there's another thing, he says, I noticed you jump very quickly to adopt these kinds of thoughts.

So? Her eyes are on him.

So you're being unfair.

Unfair?

To yourself.

How so?

If tomorrow Michelle says she loves you, that you are the best mother, would you accept that so easily?

She shakes her head. Ahh, no, no, I would think that she wants something from me, or that she doesn't yet realize the truth.

So how come you jump to the negative and away from the positive?

I don't know.

We have a rule. You cannot say I don't know.

Yes, yes, your rules.

Well?

I hate myself.

That's a slogan. Propaganda. Translate this to specific thoughts. What are you telling yourself about yourself?

I'm messed up, I'm worthless, and I'm bad, stupid.

Who says that?

I say it to myself.

Yes, but you weren't born saying that. You learned it. From whom?

From home.

Who at home?

My father.

Tell me about him.

What's to tell? Alcoholic, he beat me and slept with anything that moved. I used to hear them at night.

And you believe a person like that? You readily buy what this kind of person is selling? You base your view of yourself on this person's judgment? You base your identity on it? Your father lied. And if he didn't lie, then he was mistaken. His behavior toward you reflects on him, not on you.

I came from him.

We all came from apes. So what? Are we going to sit in a tree and eat bananas? You came from him but you are not him, and you are not his. His words hold no power over your life now. As a child you had no choice. You didn't know anything. You had no power, no perspective. You had to believe him. But you are no longer a child. You know things. And you know you are not bad and not worthless. I know this.

How, how do you know?

Would a truly bad and evil person really care to do well by anybody?

No.

Do you care to do well by your daughter?

Yes.

Does your father care to do well by anyone?

No.

So who's bad here?

My parents would fight at night. He would come to sleep in my bed. I remember when I was eleven I told my mom I was leaving home. She said OK. I remember that she helped me pack and walked me to the door. I walked to the main street, but my parents always said that I couldn't cross the main street alone, so I didn't. I stopped and couldn't go. Finally I gave up and walked back home. I felt they didn't care. I'm sure my mom watched through the window. She knew I wouldn't cross the street. How did she know that? I don't know why I didn't cross the street. What a lousy rebel I was, in the end doing everything I was told.

What you did wasn't rebellion.

It wasn't? What was it?

You say.

I don't know.

Guess.

I wanted attention.

Attention? For what? Why does a child need attention? What's attention?

I wanted her to love me.

What's that? You wanted her to say something, to do something. You wanted her to say: You are not going anywhere. You are staying here with me. You are mine. I will protect you. I will hold you.

Her head drops. Her face reddens.

And instead she helped you pack and sent you out. What did she express with these actions?

That she didn't care.

What else?

That she was angry.

Angry about what?

I don't know.

Guess.

That he came to me.

Yes.

She cries. Her shoulders tremble: He touched me, between my legs. He would say

134

it's my fault; that I bring him to this, it was pain, I remember, I didn't know anything. He said, don't say anything; it's what daddies do. Be a good girl, he said. She chokes and her voice breaks, her fingernails scratch, dig into her thighs, her knees, cutting through. My stomach aches, she says. I don't want to talk about it.

It's difficult to talk about, difficult to remember. But look where all those years of keeping silent have brought you, he says quietly. Your father is not here. And you are not a helpless child. You are protected here. You know your pain is coming from a childish place, but you are not a child anymore. You are an adult woman; a mature, strong, independent woman. And you know that problems are not resolved by avoiding them. Avoidance strengthens the problem and weakens you. If you don't confront this, then your life is still under his spell. He controls you. His violence continues. It's time to end it. Your voice has the right to be heard. Your truth has a place in the world. Your story will no longer be told by him, but by you, in your words.

He takes a small tape recorder from his desk drawer and puts it on the coffee table in front of her: Tell the truth, he says. The events you went through are over. Only the words remain. And the words cannot hurt you here.

He cannot hurt you here. Only avoidance will hurt you. I'm here with you, and I'll help you face your fears.

He would crawl into my bed, she says suddenly, he touched me, her words spill, sharp, he put his hands on my body, my chest, between my legs, patted me. He takes my hand and puts it between his legs so that I rub him there. He says, good girl, good girl. I'm crying; he puts his hand over my mouth. Shut up, he says, it's our secret, others don't understand. They don't know you like I do. She weeps, wrangles her fingers. But my mother knows, he fights with her and comes to me. I want to scream but nothing comes out. I can't breathe. He touches me, I don't know, it's like in a dream, I don't know what is happening, maybe I'm dreaming, my body is floating, like it's frozen, like a piece of wood, I don't know if it's him, it's like it's not him, it's just a blob, octopus, but his face, his face is angry, like he's in pain, and then, he breathes, he breathes on me. I remember the smell, whiskey. To this day it makes me sick. And then he gets up and walks out. I hear the door shut. I close my eyes hard . . .

She buries her head in her hands; her shoulders quiver. The psychologist waits.

Silence.

After a while he leans toward her. This entire burden your parents placed on your shoulders, he says softly, you had no choice then. Parents are normalcy for a child, they are gods; they are the world. A child does not know anything else. A child has no power, no knowledge. But now we are going to end it. The burden is theirs, not yours. You will dislodge it now. Your father hurt you and lied to you. He was responsible for your well-being, and he failed and betrayed you. Your parents' duty was to protect and nurture you. They failed. This is them and their deeds. Not you. Not your deeds. You have survived. And the goodness in you they did not erase. Say it now: I have survived.

I have survived.

I am a human being.

A human being.

Wholly human; fully human.

Wholly and fully human.

Not half-human, not subhuman.

Not half-human. Not subhuman.

And there is good inside me. There's a glowing ember of goodness.

There's good in me, an ember.

He raises his index finger in front of her eyes, a bit above them. Focus your gaze on my finger, he says quietly, when it touches your forehead your eyes will close and you will settle into a state of deep relaxation and attentiveness. He moves his finger slowly toward her forehead. Her eyes track his movement. He touches her gently between her eyes. Let your eyes close, he says. And listen to my voice. My voice will guide you. All else is just meaningless background noise. You are attentive to my voice alone. Now see this burning ember, the core of your goodness. In your mind's eye envision it glowing. Feel its warmth, see its beauty. That's the ember, your strength and good-ness. Let's strengthen it; take a deep breath and blow on it, gently: ffff . . . fffo.

Good. Now see it in your mind's eye, heating up, brightening, warming you up, bringing light in. Let those feelings of warmth and light and peace engulf you. Bathe in the light. Feel yourself relaxed. These feelings are yours. They are from you. They are in you, forever. Eternal flame. And you can return to this place, this protected place when you need to, if the world is cold, if the world is harsh. You can come back here and replenish your strength. Now repeat after me: Every day, in every way, I get stronger and stronger.

Every day in every way, I get stronger and stronger.

Repeat this twenty times.

Every day in every way, I get stronger and

stronger. Every day in every way, I get stronger and stronger. Every day in every way, I get stronger and stronger. Every day in every way, I get stronger and stronger. Every day in every way, I get stronger and stronger. Every day in every way, I get stronger and stronger. Every day in every way, I get stronger and stronger. Every day in every way, I get stronger and stronger. Every day in every way, I get stronger and stronger. Every day in every way, I get stronger and stronger. Every day in every way, I get stronger and stronger. Every day in every way, I get stronger and stronger. Every day in every way, I get stronger and stronger. Every day in every way, I get stronger and stronger. Every day in every way, I get stronger and stronger. Every day in every way, I get stronger and stronger. Every day in every way, I get stronger and stronger. Every day in every way, I get stronger and stronger. Every day in every way, I get stronger and stronger.

Now I will count to three and your eyes will open slowly and you will feel relaxed and safe. One, two, three . . .

She opens her eyes slowly. She is silent for a long time. She collects her legs under her on the sofa.

How do you know I have goodness in me?

You ask because you don't believe me?
Probably. Yes.
It's hard for you to believe me but easy to believe your drunk, scummy father?
How do you know I have goodness in me?
It's visible.

She sits quietly.

We have to finish for today, he says.
She remains curled up on the sofa, staring at him. Her eyes are soft and open wide. Her face shines suddenly in a new light. The air between them is suddenly stirred as if by an invisible hand. His breath halts, as if his body has intuited a shift that his brain has yet to process. She rises from the sofa and walks to him. Her scent, sharp and sweet, surrounds him.
Hold me, she whispers, take me, hug me.
For a moment he is frozen in his chair. He looks up at her. She stands over him, too close, her hips at his eye level. For a moment his senses blare, he melts, his head spins. Then he gathers himself, steadies his gaze on her face, gets up and walks to the door.
This session is over, he says firmly. You need to leave now.

He calls Nina.

Dr. Michaels, her voice shines.

Dr. Michaels, he says, a minute of your time?

For you, two minutes.

There was an event with the stripper today.

During session?

Yes.

An outburst, sexual or aggressive?

Sexual. She went back to her childhood trauma. Did some chimney sweeping. Let out things, and then I did a simple hypnotic induction, to strengthen her. She went with it, and then suddenly she's standing over me, asking for a hug.

Nina sighs: What do you think, a borderline loss of boundaries, fantasy play, or an attempt to sabotage treatment?

Unclear. It seems that this is the language she knows, her mother tongue, or in her case, father tongue, he says.

How did you feel?

How did I feel? Lousy.

And now?

Now we are talking, so much better.

Did you check yourself?

In what sense?

Maybe you flirted with her. Maybe you teased.

No. I'm aware. She doesn't bring that up in me.

What does she bring up in you?

Other things. Paternal feelings, perhaps.

You implied her father abused her sexually.

Yes, that's what she said.

Perhaps that's the switch. She brought up paternal feelings in you. Perhaps she sensed that vibe and reacted accordingly.

Accordingly?

Think, genius, her father sexualized the father-child relationship. A father-child dynamic emerged in therapy with you. How would she react?

Interesting hypothesis. I'll have to think about it.

You are her psychologist, not her dad.

I get it. Thanks, you have helped me. I owe you.

Likewise.

He's silent.

What's next? she says.

We'll see. I haven't decided yet. Either way we'll have to process it. Perhaps a door has opened here.

Watch out for ego.

I'm no longer there.

There's a sucker around every poker table. If you look around and don't see the sucker, it's you.

I don't play poker. I'm not a gambler by nature, but thanks.

Make sure you document everything. Protect yourself here.

Right.

And don't work harder than her.

Right.

And call me, if needed.

If needed. And if desired?

If needed and if desired, she says. Bye. And she hangs up.

He leafs through the four o'clock client's file. How can he verify whether she's telling the truth? How can he know that her story is not a contrivance, conscious or otherwise? And is it important? Years ago he treated a boy who called himself Vlad the Impaler. The kid's mother, a stocky woman with close-cropped hair and chapped lips, told him that the boy had been slaughtering the neighborhood pets, that he bled them in strange nighttime rituals and buried them in the backyard. The psychologist asked for her permission to visit their house and dig in the yard, and indeed, among the rusted trucks, tire piles, and refrigerator carcasses he found a row of cat skeletons with twisted jaws, a few patchy skinned headless rats, a luckless squirrel. Some things can and should be verified. And still, a human story's significance cannot be measured by the sum of its facts. A person, in telling of himself, at once constructs and describes his own internal architecture, which has rules of its own, chief among them the absence of clear demarcation between what happened and what didn't happen. In this inner territory the lie and its motives and processes are themselves valuable truths.

And there are things that elude explanation; slippery, highly charged eels of meaning: A father who tormented one child but spoiled the other. A father whose behavior, though normal on its face, was still experienced as hurtful by a highly sensitive child. And we have no access to the psychic genome. We cannot biopsy a child's thought as we would his skin, or organs, and decode the secrets of his mind. Were it possible to biopsy the emotionally injured and examine their tissue, to prove beyond doubt that a certain hurt is traceable to a certain person; were it possible to perform a geologic analysis of the spirit, to show that such and such hurt occurred precisely twenty-five years ago, and the other one just last week; this scar was caused by insult, that one from neglect; were it possible to construct a satellite-based GPS system that would reveal the exact location of a certain memory and its path through time, locate the source of a certain belief, a perception; were it all possible . . . but it is not. In trying to map the depths of the internal realm, all we have at our disposal are primitive tools: conversation, observation, introspection. And even with all our tools, we are lucky to ever break through even the outermost layer.

This time she shows up early. She sits in the waiting room and stares into space. At four o'clock he ushers her in. She sits down in front of him. Her body language, which is usually scattered and loose, is now zipped up like a suitcase packed for a long trip. He catches her eyes in his.

I wanted to thank you, he says.

Thank me?

Yes. What you did last time was harmful. You know this already. You did something that was hurtful to you and me and could sabotage our work and hinder your progress. At the same time, I feel that your outburst was in a way an expression of trust. I think that if you didn't trust me to handle it properly, you would not have let yourself act as you did. This trust I want to accept as a gift. And I hope to justify your faith in me. I will do everything in my power to be worthy. We cannot have a love relationship here. We cannot have a sexual relationship. But we can have trust, and mutual respect, and acceptance and understanding. That we can have.

Tears.

Silence in the therapy room.

Lingering silence.

Wrenching silence.

The sound of her breathing.

I don't know what happened to me, she says finally.

All your emotions and feelings are allowed here, he nods and leans in. You don't need to deny, suppress, or feel ashamed of your emotions, and we can study them here, we can figure them out, as we proceed. What is important now is that you see how your emotions are information, an important source of information, but not the only source. You receive information also from your life experience, and from your values and goals and future ambitions. Whatever the emotions — as an autonomous person, a human being — the choice of how to behave, how to move in the world, is always yours. And when you try to decide, to choose your steps, it's important to take into account all the information, not just the emotional piece. Do you see what I mean?

She nods weakly.

Imagine that you're walking down the

147

street with Michelle and suddenly a large, menacing dog shows up on your path. What will you feel?

Fear.

Right, and will you toss your daughter aside and run away?

Never.

Why not? That dog is really scary.

I have to protect my daughter.

Says who?

I say.

What inside of you makes you feel this way?

My love for her.

And if you were walking with some neighbor's child, would you leave it and run then?

No.

Because . . .

You don't desert a child.

You don't desert a child; what do you mean by that?

That's my belief. That's what I think.

It's a value of yours.

Yes.

And this value makes you act against the feelings of fear, to stay and protect the child.

Yes.

Which means that there are situations where we act against our feelings' recommendations, and that doesn't negate our feelings and does not diminish our humanity, but to the contrary, our humanity is then affirmed.

Yes.

This is the situation here, between us. In session, many emotions will come up, and you'll have to contain them, understand and accept them without acting on them.

Yes. Protect the child, she mumbles.

They are silent.

He turns to the desk drawer and pulls out his little tape recorder.

This is yours, he says; your story in your words, as you told it to me last week. I copied it a few times over on this tape. I want you to sit at home by yourself and listen to this tape three times every day. He hands her a sheet of paper with a table printed on it. At the end of each run, record your feelings here, your anxiety level.

I don't know, she whispers, I'm scared.

Yes, he says. A part of you is scared, and that's the signal to confront it. Avoiding fear does not solve the problem of fear but adds to it the problem of avoidance. You know this already. You are an anxiety hunter. And this tape, the memories it speaks, are only words. Words are not events. Imagine that when you were little a dog had attacked you. Back then, the dog was bigger and stronger than you. And since then you have been avoiding dogs. Even the word *dog* may scare you because you associate it with that childhood dog. But that dog is gone, and you are no longer a child. And the word *dog* does not bite. If you let the word continue to scare you, it's as if you're still back there, a scared little child, and that dog, which is actually small, and actually gone, is still menacing you and controlling your life. Do you see?

I see.

Words are not events. They represent events. But sometimes we begin to relate to a word as if it was the event itself, and if the event was painful, we try to avoid using the word that represents it. The problem is that this strategy doesn't work.

What do you mean?

First, if you're trying not to think of something, you must think about it. Let's say I told you not to think of a pink elephant; whatever you do, you must not think of the pink elephant. What will happen then?

I will think of the pink elephant.

Yes. The effort to avoid is exhausting, and unsuccessful, and injurious, because if you decide to avoid one word, with time you begin to avoid the things that remind you of it, and so you lock yourself eventually in a prison of avoidance. Because this is the truth of the internal realm: avoidance and escape are not solutions; they are the problems. If you are unwilling to feel something, to think something, then you will by definition feel and think that very thing. The way to neutralize the pain associated with a certain word, a certain memory, is to move toward it; to accept it; to embrace it; to realize that these are words, noise, and movement of the lips. No word can ever hurt you more than a habit of avoidance will. Let's practice, then. Take the word *milk*. Tell me, what does it represent?

Milk is food; it's a drink; liquid that comes from mother to feed her baby. Also cows have it.

How does milk look?

White, sticky when it dries. With a sour smell.

OK, that's milk. The word *milk*, on the other hand, is just noise, a sound that emerges from your throat through the lips. The word *milk* is not liquid and does not feed anybody. To experience this, repeat the word *milk* now for one minute straight. Focus on the sound and on the movement of your lips.

You want me to just say, milk milk?

Yes.

For what?

Try and see.

Milk milk milk milk milk milk milk milk
milk milk milk milk milk milk milk milk milk
milk milk milk milk milk milk milk milk milk
milk milk milk milk milk milk milk milk milk
milk milk milk milk milk milk milk milk milk
milk milk milk milk milk milk milk milk milk
milk milk milk milk milk milk milk milk milk
milk milk milk milk milk milk milk milk milk
milk milk milk milk milk milk milk milk milk
milk milk milk milk milk milk milk milk milk
milk milk milk milk milk milk milk milk milk
milk milk milk milk milk milk milk milk milk
milk milk milk milk milk milk milk milk milk
milk milk milk milk milk milk milk milk milk
milk milk milk milk milk milk milk milk milk
milk milk milk milk milk milk milk milk milk
milk milk milk milk milk milk milk milk milk
milk milk milk milk.

OK. Stop.

She breathes heavily.

That's the word *milk*. Sound and lip movement, he says. That's all.

He hands her the small tape recorder.

These too — just words. Three times a day, every day; listen and you'll get stronger.

A fierce debate has been raging in our field about the client as reporter, the psychologist says to the class. A classic example is of course when a client tells of some memory that has emerged during therapy, a childhood event that has floated suddenly into consciousness like a decaying body from the bottom of the river of forgetting. For years now, one camp has been urging us to accept the client's story on its face, wholly and unconditionally, to maintain the empathy and rapport that are so crucial to therapeutic success. The other camp points to memory's foibles and quirks, its spotty reliability, its proclivities toward distortion, confusion, and illusion — of which we have already spoken. Each side and its arguments, each an important voice in the conversation, but neither resolves the fundamental question: how should we hear the client's story?

The psychologist stops and waits. His gaze floats around the room and settles on the pink-haired girl. What do you think?

Ahh, I'm not sure.

Wise answer, the psychologist says. First,

the theoretical argument should stay out of the therapy room. In the therapy room we have a human encounter, not a theoretical debate. Second, if you wait until the theoretical issue is settled, then you'll wait forever. We cannot know everything. We can only know what is knowable, and we are far from mapping even that limited horizon. That's why waiting for perfect understanding and clarity before diving into the therapeutic waters is like waiting for the perfect woman before getting married — both represent fear of a real human encounter. So, you've dived in. You are sitting in front of your client. What then?

He looks around him. Silence.

$\star$ $\star$ $\star$

First, he says quietly, is humility. When you sit with your client you must remember that the science of psychology cannot predict an individual's fate. We can predict the behavior of groups. We can predict that suicide rates in a group of depressives will be higher than among nondepressives. But we cannot know which of the depressives will kill themselves. The person in front of you, his fate and his destiny are unknowable, and will remain so regardless of how much you persist and labor.

Second, the therapeutic encounter is at the core a means to an end. A weekend get-together with friends may be its own reward, an end in itself, and need not go anywhere. But therapy is not friendship, and the therapeutic encounter must move; it must go somewhere.

Go where? the pink-haired girl asks.

This you must ascertain and negotiate with the client, before and during treatment. But in every situation, the good psychologist always attends to movement, to the wind in the sails; always seeks, like a surfer, to catch the good wave and exploit its momentum. The sole purpose of every thought, every utterance, every gesture you produce in the therapy space is to advance the client's agenda: to listen to the client, to understand the client, to allow a protected space for his explorations, to share with him your knowledge of the inner architecture, to train him in the proper use of the psychological tools. All the materials of the therapeutic encounter, all its expressions and gestures exist for one legitimate purpose: discerning their role in the process of the client's healing. That's why if the client tells me, you're a fool, an uncaring son of a bitch who doesn't understand shit, I must not feel insulted, rise in defense of my honor, curse him back or abandon him in favor of a more pleasant person. All the above are legitimate responses toward friends, lovers, relatives, or strangers, but not toward the client. My greatest obligation in the therapeutic encounter is to explore how these sentiments have emerged, how they can help me understand the client better, and how I can leverage them as part of the process of helping the client heal.

Personally, if someone says this crap to me I'd smack him, Eric says, client or no client.

An almost imperceptible shudder slithers across the pink-haired girl's back. She caresses the back of her neck.

Perhaps, the psychologist says, but then your encounter is not therapeutic, and not quite suffused with humility.

Sometimes a nice whack to the head is a very effective therapy, Eric mumbles, in my humble opinion, of course.

The psychologist smiles: Notwithstanding Eric's ground-and otherwise-breaking approach, for now we choose to meet the client with humility and purpose, to try to understand her story. Alas, here we should beware, because the client will always begin with her alibi, not her story, even though her very presence at your office is evidence that her alibi has been ineffective. We do what we know. And people know their alibi much better than their story;

156

since one's alibi has daily uses while one's story — who wants it? Moreover the client's story, because it is human, contains painful elements, territories of failure and disaster. Naturally, she will seek to distance herself from these and keep away others as well, for self-protection, or out of compassion or good manners. And that's the job of the alibi: to deny, to distract and conceal and in doing so make life more bearable for the client and those around her. So your eventual work in therapy will be to walk the client from alibi to story; from the headline to the event itself. But first, the client's alibi also allows them to test you.

Test what? the pink-haired girl asks.

Two things: whether you'll buy the alibi, in which case you're useless, and whether, if you refuse to buy it, you'll resent the client for offering it, in which case you're dangerous.

You're cynical, Jennifer says.

Not necessarily. Perhaps clear-eyed. The first thing your client says is always a lie in essence, always impure. And this is not to condemn the client. Distorting and hiding the truth are, after all, essential life skills. Thus digging for truth in the context of therapy does not involve rejecting the lie, tarnishing the lie or getting rid of it, but rather a deeper acceptance and understanding that includes the lie. Therapy is not a journey from lie to truth, from darkness to light, but an attempt to find the right balance between them. That's why it is important to grasp the value of the lie and its uses.

Uses? the pink-haired girl says.

The lie, for one, is grease in the spokes of social existence, he says, where friction is high and fires may break out. Let's say I'm walking down the street and I happen across an acquaintance. We embark on a well-known dance. I'll ask, how are you? He'll say, I'm good. I'll say, long time no see. He'll say, I'll call. And we say good-bye. A well-known dance; and what's at its core?

Good manners, the pink-haired girl says.

Manners made of what?

Lies, she says with some effort.

Of course. I am not really interested in how he's doing, and he's not necessarily doing well at all, and we both know that he won't call. Still both of us went through this elaborate dance, so vacuous and yet so necessary in keeping the social peace. The naked truth, like the naked body, is a startling, charged presence, and so it must commonly be covered up. This is why you will teach your children to put their clothes on and think before they speak.

He stops and looks around.

The lie, it turns out, is not a bug in our software, but a feature of our hardware. And the good psychologist must get to know it, learn its ways.

The boy with the tie raises his hand. With all due respect, he says sternly, I hear your explanations, but I personally think that there is another path, the path of truth, and I choose to walk it, in the footsteps of my Savior.

The psychologist turns to him. Look around you, he says quietly. So many saviors, so little salvation.

At the end of class he collects his papers, stuffs them under his arm and steps out into the frozen evening. The streetlights illuminate his path to the parking lot. Snowflakes swirl around him, floating about aimlessly, as if distracted. The campus is sleepy and quiet. The psychologist winds his way to his car, trudging in the accumulating snow. He bites a mitten off his right hand, searches his pocket for the keys and leans over the door, opens it with a screech and sits down, groaning, breathing white mist at the window. He shakes off white powder from his coat and turns the key in the ignition. A squeaky cry rises from the engine's rusty depths, and then a clicking noise. He turns the key again, and this time he hears a murky cough, a faint whistle, and the engine gives up and dies. The psychologist sighs and drags himself out of his seat. He walks around the treacherous jalopy. A sudden gust of wind knocks him backward and burns his face. He finds his balance and looks around. By the edge of the parking lot he sees the headlights of an approaching car. His gaze follows the lights.

No point yelling, and also inappropriate. The car is too far to run after. As he debates his options in his head the car suddenly stops, turns, and heads toward him, its wheels splashing bits of ice around. The car stops beside him, the window rolls down, and above the loud thump of a heavy bass he hears a familiar voice: Need help, Professor?

Eric, he says, right man at the right time. I think my battery is dead.

Let's check it out. The husky youngster slides out of his seat, claps his hands several times, and his voice rises and fills with sudden, purposeful glee. Pop the hood, he says. He walks around to the front of the car, lifts the hood, and takes a small flashlight from his coat pocket. He leans into the engine, humming a joyful tune to himself. Serious junker, Professor, he says. I thought with your salary you could afford something newer. But yes, used cars, you are probably into that. He snickers to himself, smiling in the solitude of his communion with the engine.

OK, he says finally, we need a rock.

A rock?

Yes, he says merrily, there by the bushes, bring me a rock, if you will.

The psychologist walks to the edge of the parking lot, digs out a medium-size rock and

161

carries it to Eric. Eric straightens up, grabs the rock in his hand, smiles broadly and says, OK, sit inside, and when I say go, turn the key.

The psychologist obeys. Eric leans under the hood and hits something in there, once and again with a muffled thud. Finally he steps back and says, now, Professor, go.

The psychologist turns the key, and to his surprise — and not to his surprise — the engine comes to life with a yawn and a blink, an apologetic sneeze and a short bark. Eric pumps his fist in the air, yells a self-congratulatory exclamation, and proceeds to drop the hood.

The psychologist approaches to congratulate him, and extends his hand. Thank you, he says to the heavily breathing youngster, you saved me here.

It's nothing, really, Professor, Eric smiles. But maybe you should think about upgrading your wheels. He nods toward the humming car. Anyway, it was a good class. I like your vibe. I dig it.

Thanks, the psychologist says, yes, dig . . . I'll see you next week. He turns slowly toward his car.

Eric scratches his head: One more thing, Professor, since we're already here.

The psychologist turns around: Yes, sure.

It's about Jennifer.

Jennifer?

She's not like us, Professor.

Like us?

She takes things to heart. She's, you know, sensitive. You know, the things you say, she doesn't . . . she doesn't always get the humor.

Have you spoken to her?

No, no — he stomps his feet on the ground, rubs his palms together — we don't really know each other; she's not my type, and I'm in the dorms anyway, but I sit behind her, and you can see things from the back. You know.

Thanks, Eric, I appreciate the heads-up.

Yeah, no, I just wanted to let you know, you have to deal with a whole class; you can't always see everything. But I'm cool with it; I feel your game, Professor.

I see. Thanks, really.

No problem, Professor. He turns and gathers his large frame into his car, revs it up and careens away.

On the way back to his apartment the psychologist thinks about Eric, and a sudden pleasant wonderment floods him. His thoughts meander back to his class, and as he imagines his sleepy students in their chairs he feels a certain sudden queasiness. This whole educational enterprise that in the past seemed so promising and challenging suddenly feels dry and wilted. The skeleton of therapy, which he labors to construct for them, by its nature is a skeleton still, and hence lifeless, dead. Dry bones, he mumbles to himself, is all that's left of the juicy flesh of the human encounter after you have chewed and digested it for them.

Upon arrival at his apartment he enters the kitchen to make himself a cup of tea. As he focuses his attention on the teabag, he can hear noises outside: an engine yawns; a distant horn; voices of the metropolitan evening. He enjoys this moment of unremarkable flow that has no meaning and does not seek to have any. He lets the sounds wash over him and drift away, like shadows of clouds over the endless cornfields that surround the city.

The psychologist walks over to the kitchen cabinet, pulls out the half-empty bottle of brandy, returns to the table and pours some into his tea. He stirs his drink with a decorated silver spoon given to him years ago by a client, a tight-lipped business-woman who used to circle her children every night, touching toys and closing latches and whispering words and counting steps and turning on and off lights and opening and closing drawers and peeking through windows in a meticulous elaborate ritual that kept expanding until it started spilling out of the children's bedroom and into the living room and into the next morning and out of the house and into her car, trailing her all the way to her office where she would sit crazed and trembling at her desk, cleaning and wiping her children's pictures and setting them and resetting them on her desk in a straight line lest, if she faltered, she would instigate a calamity upon her darlings.

Perhaps his four o'clock client is ambivalent about her child — this thought occurs to him suddenly. You are focusing on her possible ambivalence regarding her stripping. But that perhaps reveals your own bias. Perhaps her whole story — I need to dance to collect money so I can get my girl back — is truth at the level of her consciousness, but underneath it writhe opposite, unconscious motives. Perhaps her interest in the child is a lighted alibi chasing away the darkness of her subterranean fears and anger. He thinks now that her life as a stripper allows her a double self-punishment: the archetypal humiliation of public nudity, and the continuing separation from her daughter. And he knows well the fundamental law of effect: a behavior that is rewarded will continue. A behavior that continues is being rewarded. The consequences of continued behavior, even if it doesn't seem so on its face, are experienced as a reward. Perhaps distance and humiliation are her home feelings, her native emotional tongue, to which she seeks to return. After all, Harlow's poor little baby monkeys would cling to their cloth mother even as she proceeded to reject and rebuff them. Even after Harlow, that bitter and stubborn genius, built all kinds of torture devices into the mechanical mother — a sudden air puff bursting into the baby's eyes, a hidden spring to shove him back violently, spikes that emerged to stab him — even facing all these, the little baby monkey would return and cling to the mother, desperate to appease her and find a way into her good graces, his eyes wide open in silent terror and primal insistence, as if her rejection were a signal for him not to leave but to redouble his efforts at ingratiation. Perhaps she too, the four o'clock client, continues, at the level of experience, to charge repeatedly at the source of her torment.

Your homework, he says.

The four o'clock client hands him a crumpled piece of paper.

He studies it intently and then looks at her warmly. You are working hard, with courage, he says. You have made progress.

In the beginning it was hard, she says. I sweated, I trembled. But I continued. Anxiety hunter, like you said. You're right. After a week I didn't get those feelings of fear.

So what came up?

Other feelings.

Such as?

Ahh . . . sadness.

Sadness, the psychologist says, that's the feeling that came up. That's the information. Let's study it. What do you do with it? Do you run away?

No.

Ignore?

No.

Deny?

No.

Then what?

Embrace it. Accept it.

Because?

Because running away from pain strengthens the pain and weakens me. Because a feeling you try to deny just sticks to you harder, like you said.

You've done some work, he says. Very good. Continue one more week, and we'll see what comes up.

She nods, bites her lip.

I want to turn to another issue, he says. You remember we spoke several weeks ago about your relations with your daughter, Michelle. You told me then that you feel like she is closer to her father, that she prefers him to you.

Yes.

And in the past we also spoke about your attitude toward your job, and you said you feel like you must dance to make money to try to get your girl back.

I won't try, I will get her back. He won't stop me, the hooligan. The court will not stop me. The fat bitch, his mom, all her tricks and connections won't stop me. The girl is mine. Everyone deserves a second chance, and I'm human, like you said. Fully human; not subhuman. Not half-human.

Right. Your heart is in the right place. You are indeed fully human with full rights, including the right to raise your child, and that's what you are working toward here. And part of this work involves improving your self-understanding. Knowledge is power. Self-knowledge is emotional power.

I'm getting stronger, she says. I feel it.

Yes, and now we need to go deeper. The human soul is complex. Things are not always as they seem. Like cows, that you can't imagine their complex stomachs by looking from the outside.

She smiles.

You say you want Michelle back, with all your heart.

Yes.

But she's not with you right now.

No, but . . .

Without getting into the reasons, he intervenes; let's look at the situation as it is now. She is not with you.

Right.

And you feel as if she loves her father more than you.

Yes, because he has . . .

Again, there are reasons, I know. But let's remain in the situation as it is.

OK.

And you dance at a nightclub.

I need the money.

Yes, everyone needs money. You bought a new car.

What's that got to do with anything?

A new car costs money.

She's silent.

He leans toward her: Tell me then, what am I trying to say?

I don't know.

He looks at her and waits.

Guess, he says.

I don't know; I don't know. She darkens: What do you want? What does this have to do with me? I need to get back on stage.

For?

So I can save money, for a lawyer, for college, to get Michelle back, to move . . .

Perhaps, but let's examine this. Things are not what they seem. If you had today all the money you need, would you leave the club tomorrow?

Yes.

Leave your known routine, your steady income, the attention, the power, a star on stage, all eyes on you, the girls at the club, your identity that you've built, the city you know?

Yes.

Move to a new place, unknown, unfamiliar, on your own, a new job, become a student, raise your child on your own, how?

She falls silent. Tears.

Tears.

170

Tears.

He leans forward: What am I telling you
here?
I don't know.
Guess.
That I'm scared. I . . . I'm lying to myself.
Scared of what?
Of leaving, of getting out.
And . . .
Of Michelle, of being a mom, a bad mom.
Yes, and what did we learn about fear?
What do we say instead of *I'm scared?*
A part of me is scared.
Yes, and the fact you have a part like that,
which is scared of change and of parenthood,
what does it say about you, that you are evil?
No.
What then?
That . . . that I'm human.
What kind of human?
Completely human. Not subhuman. Not
half-human.
Yes, and a human being needs courage to
see things in this way, to see the whole
picture, to admit it; courage and smarts, and
they are yours, from you.
Mine, from me.
His voice softens: This ambivalence you are
feeling about your child, about parenting, is

171

not a failure. It's an understandable reaction to your life experience, to your learning history, to the circumstances you emerged from; a common and understandable human reaction.

So I'm not that special, she says with half a smile.

A human being like the rest of us, he says. An understandable reaction, not your failure, not a reason for beating yourself up. This part of you that is scared, don't reject it; the wounded part, the part that is filled with doubts, don't cast it away; to the contrary, embrace it, soothe it, it is yours.

She is silent. Her hands cross her chest as she cradles into the sofa.

And another thing, he says, this ambivalence that you feel is scary and confusing, but it need not paralyze you.

I don't understand.

Your life today, it appears to me, is stuck in the patterns of the past and involves a comment on the past; a preoccupation with it.

I don't get it.

You have created a situation for yourself where others control you; others are using you under the guise of caring and guardianship. You found a situation where every night you go back to raise the ghosts of your childhood, becoming an object for the pleasure of others, as it was with your father.

I didn't think about it like that, she says.

Think about it like that now, he says.

Silence.

The corner of her eye moistens and dries.

The hum of the ceiling fan.

You're wrong, she finally says.

I'm wrong.

Yes, you're wrong. They are not using me; I'm using them.

Using them.

Yes, through them I will get my child back. Her voice rises: It's true; it's true what you said before. I . . . I'm scared . . . A part of me is scared that I won't know how . . . that she will reject me . . . that I . . . that I'll transmit to her the poison that the snake bit into my veins, that I will transmit it to her. But I have a plan. I'm on my way. Like you said, courage, a wise leader. I will get her back. You're wrong. Because I'm her mom. She . . . she is mine, from me. Mine. Do you understand what that means?

You feel a strong urge to get Michelle back, to be her mother. And this urge overcomes your fears and your ambivalence.

Yes.

How does it overcome them?

She thinks for a minute. She fumbles for an explanation and cannot find it. Here, look. She reaches into her purse, takes out a small gold wallet, pulls out of it a tiny picture and hands it to him. A bright-haired girl, wearing a flowery dress, stares at him seriously, her head slanted a bit to the right, her right hand shading her eyes.

Michelle? he asks.

She shakes her head: me.

He nods and looks at the picture.

That's Michelle, she says, handing him another picture; a different girl, smiling, freckled, standing under a tall pine tree, wearing the same dress.

Beautiful girls, he says. Beautiful dress. A hint of a smile crosses his face.

Do you have any children? she asks suddenly.

You are asking because . . .

No reason, she says.

Yes reason, he says.

She hesitates. Her eyes drift about the room, landing finally on his: If you have children, they're lucky. You must be such a good dad.

174

This evening, on his way to class, the psychologist stops again at the library's coffee shop. He pours himself a cup, pays and heads out into the cold. Soft snow is falling, covering the pavement in a new layer of white, wiping away the tracks of past guests and setting a new clean sheet for future ones, like an efficient hotel maid. The psychologist enters the classroom, throws his dripping coat on a chair in the corner, and turns to his students: How are we doing tonight? He looks over the room, noticing that Jennifer's chair is empty. The students return a faint moan.

OK, he says, before we begin, take two minutes, turn to the person next to you and find out how they are doing. He waves his hands: Go on. They turn to each other with creaking chairs. A blare of giggles and noise emerges, charging up the room's atmosphere. The white teeth girls huddle around the boy in the tie, whose face reddens suddenly. The pink-haired girl, the psychologist notices, walks over to Eric, shows him something on her cell phone screen, and they both giggle as if sharing a secret.

OK, the psychologist finally says, you've woken up. Let us then return to the therapeutic encounter. Two fundamental aspects of the therapeutic encounter are the content and the process. The content is the *what* and the process is the *how*.

What about *why*? Eric mumbles.

Why is a weak question, fuzzy, and lacking a precise answer. The good psychologist will stay away from the *why* question.

Why? Eric giggles.

You got it, the psychologist says. Let's understand that the client's problem involves either content or process. A client who cannot get sexually aroused by a specific woman has a content problem. A client who's afraid of sexual feelings in general has a process problem. Philosophically, we'll agree, the distinction is murky and problematic, but a preoccupation with theory constitutes an avoidance of the therapeutic work. Most prolific scientists know little about the theory of science. In the therapy encounter, the beads of content are usually strung together on a transparent but strong string of process, and the psychologist would do well to inquire about not only the single beads but also the type of string that holds them together.

Let's take the following case: a client comes

in for treatment of anxiety. She's a single woman in her thirties. She sees her boyfriend mostly as a friend and is not attracted to him sexually and is never orgasmic. She lives with her parents. She enjoys coaching the local high school's cheerleader squad. She describes episodes of magical narcissistic thinking where she imagines she can foresee the future, and that others around are talking about her. All these symptoms differ at the level of content, but on the process level they are all arranged on one invisible string and express, if we take a somewhat Adlerian perspective, a fear of growing up, a process of refusal to mature.

Now, young therapists spend much time worrying about therapy content: what's the right thing to say at any given moment. This attention to content, while valuable, still misses the role of process. The good psychologist knows that change, any change within known boundaries, is in itself therapeutically valuable because it shakes up the rug, ruffles up existing systems, and provides a new experience. Presenting a new tack demonstrates to the client that new tacks exist, and expresses implicitly a stance of courage toward the world: experimentation is allowed. A shake-up, any shake-up, yields important information about the client, about their ways of handling novelty. The process of intervening may affect the client regardless of the content of a given particular intervention. Now let's practice. Here's a couple in the middle of a dialogue. Where are they?

In the bedroom, Jennifer, who had sneaked into her chair, says quietly.

That's a physical *where*. Where are they mentally?

Engaged, she says. They are in a relationship, a young couple.

Yes. That's a social and psychological *where*. What's the content?

She's mad . . .

Mad is not *what*; it's *how*. What is she saying? What are her words?

She is saying: It's my day, and I want white roses on every table. Maybe that's not important to you, but it matters to me. And if it's important to me, it should also be important to you. We're getting married, if you haven't noticed. I'm on the phone all day and there's one little thing that matters to me, that I want, and suddenly there's no more money. There's money to fly in your friend from Vermont, who by the way happens to be your ex-girlfriend's brother; there's money for that but not for roses . . .

Yes, that's the content. What's the process?

Divorce proceedings, Eric mumbles under his breath.

The pink-haired girl giggles quietly.

What is the process?

Conflict, Jennifer says in almost a whisper. She pulls absent-mindedly at the wrists of the sleeves that cover her thin arms. The psychologist notices the gesture and marks it to himself.

More basic, he insists.

They are in a dialogue, she says.

More basic.

Monologue.

What kind?

Self-examination, Jennifer says.

More specific.

Self-doubt.

Yes, the psychologist says, smiling at her. You are beginning to hear the music. Our commerce with the world is always in some form a reflection of our commerce with ourselves. He turns to the class. Jennifer has courage, he says. Jennifer has discovered something about herself here. Thanks, Jennifer. She looks at him aghast, as if she has suddenly realized for the first time the meaning of her words.

It is important, then, to tend to content and process, he continues. And at the same time we should also attend to how our clients frame their issues, how the client defines the problem to himself. What lens does he use to capture the scene? Note that if you zoom in, even a small group of fans will fill the screen and hence, in your mind, the whole stadium. But if you zoom out, you will notice that the stadium is empty but for a small, rowdy group of devotees. The meaning of the situation changes completely. Let's suppose, Eric, that you are a slave and unhappy about it. How will you frame your predicament? You could tell yourself, I need to find a kinder master. Or you could say, I need to be free, be my own master. The way you define your problem will determine the direction of your efforts, and hence the course of your life. That's why it's important to help the client seek a better, more useful and compassionate frame. The meaning of any event emerges from how it's framed. Here you are, Eric, coming back home at two o'clock in the morning from a night on the town with your pals. Your wife is waiting at the door, upset.

Wow, you got me married, Eric protests.

We're talking potential scenarios, even though statistically speaking it's plausible that you'll find your future wife around here, in this town, or in this college, perhaps even in this class, since it is an empirical fact that we select a partner who resembles us and who is usually from somewhere nearby. People are not magnets and opposites do not attract, at least not in the long run — but I got carried away. Where was I?

Eric came home late and his wife is mad, Jennifer says.

Yes, Eric. You came in late and you didn't call. Your wife says that you are selfish and uncaring. You reply, you're controlling and not trusting; why don't you give me some space? Here we have a struggle. Two competing frames are doing battle, and the one who defines the event, who frames it, will win the war because every battle from then on will happen on their terms. This struggle for framing reality is going on all around us all the time and on every level. Lottery proponents say, you may win millions. Lottery opponents say, you will likely lose everything you put in. The pharma company says, the medicine has a seventy percent success rate. Antipharma people say, it has a thirty percent failure rate.

He turns to the pink-haired girl: Suppose I offer you a deal. I'll give you a technology that will make you rich, will make your life better, will make everyone's life better, will make this country an economic powerhouse, and will upgrade all our lives immeasurably. All I ask in return is that you let me come in once a year, pick forty thousand people at random, and kill them. Do we have a deal?

No, she says. No way! I'm not a killer.

Of course. Another question: are you willing to give up your car right now, give it up for good?

No way.

Of course not. But here's the problem: the deal you just rejected is in fact your car. The invention of the car upgraded all our lives, and every year forty thousand people die because of car accidents.

Her face falls.

Tricky, Eric says.

The frame, the definition, is a type of context. And context, as we said before, determines the meaning of things. There is no such thing as the view from nowhere, or from everywhere for that matter. Our point of view biases our observation, consciously and unconsciously. You cannot understand the view without the point of view. He walks to the computer, fiddles with it, and a picture emerges behind him on the screen.

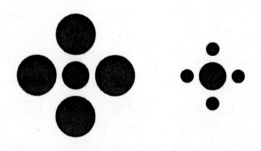

He waves his hand: Which center circle is larger? The eye, or to be precise, the brain — because we see with our brain, not with our eyes — anyway, the brain thinks the larger circle is on the right. But if we measure, that is, if we take the scientific approach, we will find that the center circles are identical. In this case, as in many others, the context disorients the brain. If we grasp the client's context, we can grasp what disorients him.

⋆　⋆　⋆

When class is over, the psychologist collects his papers, leans over his desk and turns off the computer. His students hurry to leave, scattering quickly into the darkness as is the custom of students everywhere. Only the boy in the tie remains sitting at his desk. He appears to be asleep, but his lips are moving. He is praying silently, his hands clenched at his chest. The psychologist stands up. The boy in the tie turns his head slowly. Their eyes meet.

Everything OK? the psychologist asks.

The boy in the tie looks at him intently. No, he says finally.

Can I help?

Thanks, but I have help; my Lord and

Savior, he says, and holds his right hand to his chest.

Just because you talk to him doesn't mean you can't talk to me, the psychologist says quietly.

Silence.

The boy in the tie sits upright in his chair, his lips clenched.

It must be difficult for someone like you, a believer, to attend a class like this that deals with secular issues and science . . .

My presence is important here; I have a role here, the boy says.

The psychologist nods: I am glad you decided to enroll; your perspective enriches the conversation in class. He stands and waits.

Silence.

Can I ask you a question? the boy finally says.

A question; sure.

I have this situation at home . . . you see, my folks, they are believers. And me, you know I was always the rebel; I made their lives hell in high school. I got in trouble all the time. My big brother, he was the good one, an A student, honors classes, active in the church, choir and band at school, a good boy, polite, popular. We weren't really close. We're six years apart. I admired him as a child, but I could never compete with him, so, it's no surprise to you probably, I found a different route; if you can't join them, beat them, you know . . . Anyway, after he finished college he left for California, got a job there, and since he left we became closer, we e-mail each other. He helped me, encouraged me, and told me to take care of our parents. A year ago my father got cancer. It was hard for my mother. Dad was always the strong one, you know. I sat by him, in the hospital, all year. He used to drift in and out of consciousness. Sometimes at night he would come to and whisper, Nathan. Just a whisper, but I would wake up and I'd say, I'm here. And he'd drift off again. I was with him when he died. That was when I saw the light. The Savior entered my life then. Anyway, a month ago my brother invited me for a visit. I was there for a weekend. He lives with another guy. At first I thought they were roommates, but then, you know, he confessed. He told me he always was . . . that he always felt different. They have been together for two years now, and they want to adopt a child, they want to get married, or something like a marriage, they have those ceremonies there in California. He wants me to accept him, his path. And it wasn't hard for me, actually. The Savior's compassion is for everybody; you know, we are all sinners. I'm not the judge. There's only one judge. Only He can judge. And if He took me back, then who am I to judge? But now my brother wants me to help him tell Mom. He says he's tired of hiding and deceiving. He wants her to come to their ceremony. It's important to him. He insists on it. And I understand him, really, but I don't know if Mom will be able to take it. She's a believer, old school, and she's not as strong as she was, you know; she's old. And what she had to go through . . . I don't know if it's right to dump this on her. She adores my brother, worships him. I don't think she'll be able to handle it. I've prayed over this a lot. The Good Book says, hate the sin, not the sinner. And he's my brother, he's family. He deserves to live his life, be who he is, I guess. But maybe he can wait a few years; how long does she have to live anyway? Why break her heart? He lifts his eyes toward the psychologist.

A human situation, the psychologist nods; a complex human dilemma. And you said you had a question?

What should I do? What's right to do?

I don't know, the psychologist says. But it seems to me you are approaching the question from a place of compassion.

Nathan nods slowly.

If you come from that place, perhaps any decision you make will be the right one.

The boy nods; his face softens.

Thank you, he says. And if I may, it's important for me to say that you are a nonbeliever, I know, but the spark of the divine is inside you too. And His love, His path, is open to you too.

The psychologist smiles. Perhaps, he says, and perhaps my time has come and gone. And now it is late and time to go home. Good night, then, and I'll see you next week.

The next morning, driving down the street on his way to work, the psychologist glimpses an old beat-up piano standing on a neighbor's lawn. A sign is taped to it: *Free to a good home*. The psychologist stops his car at once, gets out and walks over to the huge instrument, walks around it, strokes it with his hand. It seems to him suddenly that this piano on the lawn at the side of the road, despite its menacing bulk, despite its severe color, is like an abandoned, lost child. Its presence here on the lawn seems like a terrible mistake, or perhaps on the contrary, a grand and surprising opportunity. A powerful, unexplainable urge rises in him suddenly. He knocks on the door of the neighbor's house and a young man, half-naked and rumpled from sleep, peeks out, rubbing his eyes.

Your piano? the psychologist asks.

The man nods: We're moving. I got a job in Seattle. It belongs to my wife's mother. We don't play. She moved to a retirement home, so we took it. It must be a hundred years old.

Scratches and cracks are etched in the old

piano's body. It looks like a monument to something, some lost beauty, an unfulfilled promise. Again you see metaphors around you, the psychologist thinks to himself; but this piano is too concrete a presence, standing upright, somber and stubborn and quiet like a dead tree; and even though it is falling apart, a certain light still emanates from it, a wholeness.

Will you help me push it to my place? the psychologist asks. I'll pay you twenty bucks.

They grab and push the massive body; the wheels underneath squeak and groan, shaking off an ancient, thick coat of rust. Stutter-stepping and heaving, they cross the street and the cement pavement and up the two stairs that lead to the psychologist's door. The neighbor sighs and wipes the sweat off his brow. The psychologist is overcome by a strange giddiness; he feels childlike and drunk. They labor mightily to drag the echoing heap of wood and iron through the narrow doorway. One of the wheels gives up abruptly, twists off, and scratches the wooden floor in protest, leaving behind an unsightly scar. But the psychologist pays no heed. This piano, reluctant to budge as it is, does not appear stubborn to him but rather unconscious, fallen in a faint. Another shove and push, and the piano now leans against the living room wall, tilting some to the right, its massive bulk lording over the cramped confines of the small room. The psychologist offers the neighbor some cash. The neighbor declines and leaves. The psychologist sits in his chair and observes his treasure. The piano, it now becomes evident, is too big for the space, but it projects an easygoing, benevolent air. The psychologist gets up and approaches the beast. He lifts the dusty, stained cover and bangs on the yellowish keys. *Find piano tuner*, he jots down in his little pad.

I got a piano, he tells Nina a few days later, sitting in his office, his legs resting on his desk.

You bought a piano?

I found a piano.

Found?

A neighbor decided to get rid of it. I was driving down the street and I saw it on the lawn. Something happened. I could not leave this piano alone there. It felt like leaving a baby on the street. I had to adopt it.

Why don't you adopt a dog?

I don't like dogs. They cling. They are noisy. They shed.

A cat?

Cats are too self-satisfied. They run from room to room for no reason at all. It makes me tense.

A bird?

Birds should fly freely. A caged bird is depressing.

Goldfish? she laughs.

What are you? A missionary? He gets angry: You are not listening. What's wrong with a piano?

You are distancing yourself from people, from life, systematically. You've adopted an object.

A piano is not an object. This piano definitely isn't. If you see it, you'll understand. A tide of resentment swells inside him.

I'm happy for you that you'll get back to playing. Actually, I never got to hear you play.

You didn't miss much. What I lack in technique I make up for in sentimentality.

I would like to hear you play.

Well, my apartment is open to you, although now there's no more room because the piano is taking up all the space.

She laughs. What about our stripper?

She's working. She's very focused on her daughter.

She has a daughter? From whom?

Her ex. He abused her during the pregnancy, she says. He got custody. She was into drugs back then.

Believable story?

Perhaps. I'm not the police. Either way

she's locked in on this issue.

What issue?

To get her daughter back. That's her compass. Everything goes back to that for her.

And what's your take?

It's a genuine motivation; it could become a therapeutic leverage. I'm feeling around for that.

Don't forget there's another side to this.

What side?

The girl. The girl's best interest.

Yes, but the girl is not my client.

Don't be a wiseass.

Yes. No. OK, I got it.

In his ear he hears a loud beep, and then another one. I got another call, he says, we'll talk later.

Bye.

He presses the talk button: Yes? A voice is heard, a sharp, high-pitched, unfamiliar voice: Are you Tiffany's shrink?

I don't talk on the phone about my clients. Who's this?

Bora.

Well, Bora, personal information about therapy clients is confidential and is not discussed with strangers on the phone.

I'm Tiffany's boss.

Either way, I don't talk about my clients with strangers.

I'm not at all a stranger. Here, she'll tell you.

He hears the four o'clock client's voice, higher, more urgent than usual: It's me, Doctor. I agree. Talk to him. It's OK.

I am not speaking to anyone without permission from you.

You have my permission.

Written permission.

Please, Doctor, she pleads, just have a word. She sobs.

Put him back on.

Yes, the voice sounds.

I'm listening, Bora.

Yes. You listen. Every day Tiffany doesn't dance, I lose money.

With all due respect, your money is not my concern. My concern is my client.

Yes, yes. The voice sounds thoughtful now, but still haughty: Why with anger? I'm just asking you, sir, that you do what you can to get Tiffany back to work. Make her better so she comes back to dance.

I understand. Anything else?

That's all. I am happy we have agreement. Agreement is always better than disagreement, yes?

Thank you and good-bye.

The psychologist hangs up the phone and leans back in his chair. He notices now that his jaw feels tight, his stomach muscles cramp. Where are your feet right now? He leans back in his chair and crosses his hands behind his neck. He breathes deeply. The sudden queasiness begins to subside. He opens her file and writes down: *A man called, identified himself as Tiffany's boss. She gave verbal consent. He demanded to see progress. Aggressive tone. A threat? Explore.*

The therapeutic encounter is in essence a human event, and as such inherently paradoxical, he says to the scattered group of students in front of him, noticing that Jennifer's chair is empty again. Remember the teachings of Paul Meehl, that learned instigator: anecdote and intuition, loyal paramours of the mythological psychologist, are the enemies of the good psychologist. Enchanting yet treacherous sirens, they must not replace our workaday, systematic pursuit of evidence and cannot supplant in our alliances the known laws of the universe. The laws of gravity and probability apply to all of us equally. And so your ability to easily recall a certain event does not mean the event is common or important. And even if the creature in the bushes walks and talks and looks like a duck, you will do well to find, before declaring it a duck, whether your environment is in fact a plausible duck habitat . . . And the fact that your distant cousin on your mother's side wet his bed until age sixteen and today he's an odd loner does not establish bedwetting as the universal cause of oddity and isolation. The fact that all your clients speak of their painful chaotic childhoods does not constitute proof that all who suffer as children are doomed to adult ruin. Those who overcame their childhood hardships on their own — and they are the overwhelming majority — will not show up at your clinic, after all. The fact that most prisoners are criminals does not mean that most criminals are in prison. Here too the old Viennese stumbled, as he labored to dig up the acquired quirks and neglected to acknowledge those innate leanings of the mind; fiddled with the software and forgot the hardware. Our encounter with the client has to be, in this context, a scientific inquiry, in which we seek to raise and test hypotheses regarding the client's knots and the proper ways to untie them.

At the same time, forget Paul Meehl, he says. Your encounter with the client is a unique event, like a work of art. The client's story, bound and anchored as it is in the general laws, still amounts to a unique, concrete experience. Those who walk the same path, their pace and stride still differ, their thoughts, the trail of their gaze, differ. A man walks on the beach like a thousand before him, but in his exact footprints — their path and depth and contours — he is unique.

Even identical twins have different thoughts at any given time and cannot occupy the exact same place physically. The language of laws and generalizations cannot contain the whole of human experience. The average mother has 2.2 children, but you will not meet even one actual mother with 2.2 children. It is important to know how many millions of people have died in a particular war or atrocity, but such knowledge will not bring tears to anyone's eyes. The personal story of one casualty will. The good psychologist must be present in this place, face the client as one person facing another, not as two sides of some abstract equation, and by his presence help gather and restore the client's broken narrative, the client's identity: You are heard. Your voice resonates. You exist. You are a person, a person in the world . . .

The door opens and Jennifer walks in without looking at him. Her head hangs low. She sits in her chair, her face pale and closed.

. . . And cut the jabbering, the psychologist says, his eyes gliding over her without stopping. Everything that can be said can be said clearly, so said Wittgenstein, and you don't want to pick a fight with that guy; just ask Karl Popper, who almost caught a fireplace poker to the head in 1946 in

Cambridge. Everything that can be said can be said clearly; and succinctly, I say. Forty words, twenty seconds, that's the time you have to express yourselves in therapy. Beyond that lies the realm of speechifying; the client becomes your audience, and your speech, even if brilliant on the level of content, will be perceived by the client on the level of process as inattentiveness, or maybe even an attempt to stifle, or an inability to tolerate silence. The work of speechifying and obfuscation we shall leave, with all due respect, to academia — he slaps his chest with his palm. And no advice. For advice let them go to the Internet or to the library, or to the merest acquaintance who is always happy to offer advice on any concern. No. People do not come to the therapist's office to seek advice or hear speeches. And the question is, then, what do they come for?

Friends for hire, Eric says. My dad says that psychologists are friends for hire.

Your friends are involved in your daily life; your psychologist isn't.

But still, the psychologist listens, Eric says. People love it when someone listens to their crap. You like it when we listen, don't you?

Come again, I didn't quite catch it . . .

Eric laughs.

Attention is part of it, the psychologist

198

says, but a dog listens too. And it's free.

But a dog doesn't understand, says the pink-haired girl.

Right. Human understanding requires human attention. But your friends understand you. And so do your enemies. We're missing a fundamental ingredient. The clients are seeking an experience. What experience are they seeking, Eric?

Experience . . . experience, Eric mumbles.

A healing experience, Jennifer chimes in.

OK, the psychologist says. Somebody's done their reading. But what does that mean? What's healing in the healing experience?

Depends on what's broken. My car needs a healing experience in the carburetor, Eric says.

Let's focus on the human experience.

You said we were used cars.

That's a metaphor, Eric, and it's important to know when to let sleeping metaphors lie. Now think, what's the most basic impairment?

They stare back at him, silent.

Examine your own lives. What characterizes the basic trouble in your day-to-day?

Fears, Jennifer says finally.

Fears are a symptom, of what?

Demands, she says.

Demands? Explain.

Everybody wants something from you. Everybody judges you. Everybody.

What do they want?

My parents want me to succeed in school and my boyfriend wants me to look hot and relax, as if that's possible when you're stressed about arranging a wedding; you want us to read and prepare and answer your questions. My boss at the restaurant wants me to clear the tables faster and show up early and always smile regardless of whether the customer left a decent tip . . .

Indeed, the psychologist says, our everyday proceedings are marked by constant social judgment, and therefore constant fear of rejection, which is at bottom what?

Fear of isolation, loneliness, Jennifer says.

Yes, the psychologist says, the fear of loneliness, which is at bottom what?

Fear of death? Jennifer asks.

Indeed. Rejection leads to isolation, and isolation is death, both physically, since a newborn who's left alone will die within forty-eight hours, and psychologically, since man is a herd animal, a social animal. And herein lies the secret of the therapy experience: acceptance, genuine acceptance that does not demand anything in return; full acceptance of the client, warts and wounds and injuries and all. Such acceptance pushes back the fear of death, even if just for a while, for the therapy hour, like a flashlight's beam of light calms the person who's walking through darkness even without chasing the darkness away entirely. Acceptance allows the client to rest, allows him time and space within which to sense himself fully, sober up, look inward and around him, organize the matter of his being, tune his instruments, play the right note. Such acceptance is the life-blood of therapy, the active ingredient. And without understanding there is no acceptance.

But still, Eric says, it's conditional acceptance. Acceptance as long as the client pays.

Yes, the psychologist says, of course. On a certain level everything is conditional. Even unconditional acceptance is conditioned on the absence of conditions. And what of it? The psychologist has to eat too. The fact that you pay to see a good concert does not mean that the musicians are preoccupied only with your money; doesn't mean that their playing is coming from an inauthentic place; doesn't mean that your experience, your connection with the musicians and the music — and through them with yourself and the world — is not real. The fee is the passport. The treatment is the journey.

On his way to the gym this evening for his weekly basketball game, his loneliness reveals itself to him. A man alone in his twenties is single; alone in midlife, lonely; alone in old age, discarded. The path is clear. The psychologist turns this recognition over in his mind, attempting to feel its contours and dimensions. It appears real to him, soft and appeased, present and felt but not heavy, not burdensome. His life in its way is full. His everyday flows, peaceful and known. His nights are long and unperturbed. The young students at the college take in his lectures according to their varying abilities, and sometimes revelations sparkle like diamonds in their eyes. Sometimes his words fall like rain, and a rich harvest follows. His clients come and go, taking with them for their journeys what they may. From time to time he likens his meetings with them to a voyage in a faraway exotic land, inaccessible to most; and yet he, by virtue of his curious calling, is invited to explore the terrain with them, take in the sights. How could he complain? Perhaps he would like a bigger apartment, allowing more room for the old piano, affording him the option to entertain. But even a man with a hundred bedrooms goes to sleep every night in one bedroom. And who is there for him to entertain? He has no interest in small talk; his neighbors and acquaintances are busy with their lives, and why would he bother them? His sister, eight years his senior, lives with her husband and two children in a small town on the East Coast. His parents used to live around there. When they were alive he used to visit them once a year. But then his father died. Heart attack. Folded over in his chair, the sports section crumpled underneath him. Two years later his mother died of cancer. His sister carried the load, nursed his mother and cared for her daily while he was busy with his graduate studies. The last time he saw his mother she was already exhausted and foggy. She took his hand in hers and they sat on the living room couch. She whispered to him, I need a miracle. He sat in silence. Since the death of their parents his ties to his sister have waned. One summer a few years ago he went to visit her again, after she pleaded with him repeatedly. She took him to the beach and they walked slowly on the waterline, her children frolicking in front. I'm proud of you, of your achievements, she said. Thanks for taking care of Mom and Dad, he said. And he felt then that their closeness was like an old defunct lighthouse, standing strong but shedding no light. Once or twice a year, usually on the anniversary of their mother's death, his sister will call him and ask how he's doing. I'm doing well, he says, and she tells him of her kids, now adolescents, and says she's OK too. His boyhood friends have long ago scattered across the large continent. Their attempts to bridge the geographic divide weakened over time and were replaced by palliative, tender acceptance. His lost friends he did not manage to replace. Deep, fulfilling friendship, he has learned, is one of those enterprises unsuited to a late start, like dancing, or computer savvy.

The game flows nicely for him this evening. The ball rests comfortably in his hands. His feet are light and swift, his movements precise and timely, as if he has shed for one magical hour the clunky burden of his excess years. For a moment he forgets the accumulating evidence of his body's imminent betrayal. Toward the end of the game, excited and heaving, he charges to the basket, leaps in the air, releases the ball in a high arc toward the hoop, and as he lands, full of a sense of sweet accomplishment, he steps inadvertently on another player's foot, twists his ankle and collapses to the floor with a muffled cry. The others gather round him, their faces worried. They reach and hold out their hands to him with a known blend of compassion and impatience, eager to get back to the game. He sees it and does not begrudge them.

I'm OK, he says, go on without me. He leaves and limps to his car. His muscles ache now, as if collecting a delinquent debt. On his way back to his apartment the road is deserted and a thought surfaces in him that he could, if he wanted to, continue to drive on, beyond his apartment and on beyond the city limits and on down the endless freeway, turn this way or that, as he wishes. He's free to do as he pleases, and the road is open. On, if he wishes, to the north, a few short hours along the flat road to another town, where a woman lives with her bright-eyed daughter. He could come to their door. Wouldn't they take him in? Wouldn't they throw their arms around him? Won't his heart sing at the sight of them and open and fill with light? His head spins. Some questions are their own answers. This he should know, but he does not know right now. He gathers himself, turns right at the light onto the familiar street, parks, climbs out of his car and limps to his door.

At exactly four o'clock he goes out to the waiting room. She sits there in the corner, as is her habit. Beside her is an unfamiliar man, thin and diminutive, his hair is graying and cut short. His shoes are shining blue. In his hand he holds an unlit cigarette. The psychologist steps forward toward them. The four o'clock client lifts her eyes and he glimpses in them a sudden shadow. She stands up. The man beside her stands up as well; he steps forward quickly and holds out his hand.

Hi, he says, I'm Bora. The psychologist shakes his hand. Bora holds on to it forcefully and does not let go. So you're the shrink?

The psychologist nods.

We need to talk, the man says softly.

We can schedule an appointment, the psychologist says, looking over at Tiffany.

Now, the man says, we'll talk now. Ten minutes.

Now I have an appointment with Tiffany.

Tiffany agrees, he says and turns to her. Yes, honey? I speak with doctor ten minutes and then you continue. I pay. He taps his pocket.

206

She nods and looks at the psychologist. It's OK, she says. I'll wait here.

Are you sure?

Yes, yes. Speak to him.

The psychologist nods and leads Bora to the therapy room. Bora enters and looks around with a thoughtful expression; the corners of his mouth are upturned in a half smirk. He walks over to the shelf and takes the gold clock, examines it closely, humming to himself, his back to the psychologist. Just arrived and already he acts as if he owns the place, the psychologist thinks uncomfortably. He sits down and clears his throat. Bora places the clock gently back on the shelf and turns on his heels in a soft pirouette-like motion.

The psychologist points to the sofa: Please have a seat.

Bora sits down and waves his cigarette. No smoking? he asks and then slides the cigarette into his shirt pocket. The psychologist waits. They stare at each other.

I can't discuss clinical matters with you, the psychologist says. Tiffany will have to sign a consent form.

She'll sign, Bora nasalizes. Bring her here and she'll sign.

I don't work like this. I'll have to meet with her in confidence, alone. Signing under pressure is unacceptable as far as I'm concerned.

Pressure, what pressure? Why go . . . He measures his words, falls silent for a moment, and then the sly smile. I'm a businessman, Doctor. We both have same interest. We both want Tiffany better.

What did you want to tell me?

A minute, Doctor, no need to rush, Bora says. He leans back in the sofa. I need her on stage. She's my star. She's got it, he moves in his seat, she's got something that makes customers feel good, their money flows. The money, he scratches his chin, that's another thing; I am losing a lot of money, Doctor, and she's not dancing. I wouldn't want to see her back on the street. A pity; such talent. But I run a business, you understand, Doctor, and she is also . . . lately I think maybe she's not really sick, you understand me, Doctor. How do you know what's in here? He points to his head. She doesn't have fever. She's not bleeding. She looks healthy. I'm not a doctor or anything. I'm a businessman, but still, I got eyes, as a businessman I need to know people, you know, and I think maybe she got ideas in her head . . .

The psychologist nods. He feels a burning in his stomach. Bora's offhanded arrogance, his bearing, his patronizing of Tiffany provoke uneasiness and resentment in the psychologist. A sliver of hostility is threaded into his

208

mind. There is no vacuum in the world, he thinks bitterly. Take off your hands and someone else will put his on. With all due respect, he says, a hint of anger at the edge of his voice, her ideas are her business, and neither I nor anybody else has a monopoly on her wishes and plans. She is an adult woman and is free to choose as she pleases. Perhaps she wants a different life. She has the right to think ahead beyond now, beyond you, sir, perhaps even beyond herself — about others, if she wants. I am not a career consultant, and I don't get involved in my clients' lives. We are focused here on her stage fright, but everything is connected and there are always unknown consequences. What do you need from me?

Yes, yes, Bora says. His gaze sharpens for a split second and an involuntary tic flashes across his face. I just say, if she is sick, then cure her. That's all. It's really important. Do your job, Doctor. Get her back on the stage. Everybody benefits then, yes? You don't want her in the street. With the club she has work, money, yes? She's protected. Nobody bothers my workers, you understand. She is a star with me, yes? I picked her up from the street. She was nothing how she was then. I picked her up, cleaned her up, like my child I took care of her, yes?

Morning. The psychologist is bent over his computer keyboard in his small study; a child's picture comes on the screen, open-faced and bright eyed, hugging a pink teddy bear. He stares at the screen for a long time, breathing with effort, biting his lower lip, leaning back in his chair, and then he suddenly gets up and goes out in a rush.

He drives in silence. The radio is turned off. Heavy snow is falling. His tired wipers streak back and forth across the windshield. Large trucks plod through the muddy snow, barreling to his left and right. He holds the wheel in both hands, straining his neck to see. Six hours of driving, he calculates, and he'll be there. He found Nina's office address on the computer. He'll wait there and follow her to the kindergarten; will steal a glance at Billie, just once drink in her shining beauty and then he will turn and go home. Just one time before they leave for California. After three hours he stops at a gas station to refuel and eat. He buys a sandwich and bites into it as he drives. He calls and cancels his few appointments for the day. An hour later he looks around through the falling snow. He is surrounded by frozen fields as far as the eye can see, and for a second his confidence is lost. For a second he does not know whether he's coming or going. But then he regains his focus, searches out the road signs; he bites into an apple he brought with him and drives on. By the afternoon he's at the edge of town; a suburb like all suburbs; gas stations, fast-food joints, garages, car lots, banks; asphalt everywhere, filthy cement, and the air hums with American desolation, exhausted, sour and impatient. He glances at the directions sheet he printed earlier and makes his way onto the campus. He stops his car by the psychology department building and notices the skies have cleared. The sun shines. A cocked giddiness bubbles up in him. Two young students come out the front door and pass by him, laughing and curled in their parkas like bear cubs. A bearded man walks by, carrying a beefy brown briefcase, talking on a cell phone that is stuffed under the hood of his coat. And here she is, walking right past his car. He curls into the seat and his eyes track her. A discomfort seeps into his consciousness all of a sudden. What are you doing here? And why are you hiding from Nina? But a certain hardened stubbornness rises too, and a kind of childish excitement.

What's the matter? No harm done. A man can see his daughter, and covet his lover. A man is allowed his secrets, things between him and himself, knowledge that is not meant for sharing. A man is allowed his inner world, allowed his fantasies. Her car leaves the parking lot and he rolls behind, keeping his distance. Once in a while at a traffic light he inches nearer and can see through her back window the contours of her head, her long neck. At this sight he is reminded of her scent, the feel of her warm skin, the darkness between her thighs. His mind whirls and he almost loses her, but here she turns right into a narrow side street and stops in front of an old building surrounded by tall trees. She walks through the gate and disappears in the doorway. He waits, and here they are, a tall woman holding the hand of a small girl who's wrapped up in a red coat, a yellow scarf around her neck. They cross the street. The girl turns her head, and for one second he catches the full of her round face, her almond eyes that she inherited from her mother, her innocent smile. The girl points up with a tiny index finger. Her mother leans over and buttons her coat and they approach their car. My girl, he whispers to himself. Billie. Go home, he thinks. You saw her and she is perfect; full of life, wrapped in love. Go home.

He drives after them. The sky is clear; pristine light anoints the city. He follows them to the outskirts of town. A primordial hunter's rush bubbles up in him. They park by a small frozen pond. The sun shines brightly now. They disappear in a small building on the side and reappear a few minutes later, wearing their skates. They toddle onto the ice sheet and immediately the girl swings around, skating joyfully on the shiny ice surface, fearlessly turning and waving her hand at her mother, motioning her to follow. Nina moves cautiously, leaning forward slightly, her hands spread at her sides for balance. At the sight of her body a shiver slithers along his spine; longing and lamentation swirl about him like music. He gets out of his car, walks to the edge of the ice and stands under a naked tree, his palm over his forehead, shielding his eyes from the sun. Billie dances around in circles and figure eights, her arms waving as she glides lightly, gathers up speed. His heart glides with her, and he mouths, watch out little girl. Careful. Don't fall. Careful, my little child. Nina appears, she bends and gathers the cub in her arms, and they both turn and fall to the ice laughing. He steps forward unwittingly. A group of adolescent boys skates right in front of him, hockey sticks at the ready, chasing an elusive puck, bumping into each other with a great ruckus. When his gaze lifts again he sees Nina standing frozen, staring straight at him with a look of disbelief, the girl wrapped around her ankle. He stands still; he does not feel remorse or fear. Only calm, a merciful calm envelops him, envelops the two figures gliding in his direction, the rowdy boys in the distance, and the whole glistening pond. He waits. Nina and Billie, hand in hand, are now standing in front of him. Silence.

Nina gathers herself: It's really you.

It's really me.

I can't believe this. What are you doing here?

Ahh, he stumbles, that's a good . . .

Everything OK?

Ahh . . .

She looks in his eyes, and her stare is like a canvas on which too many colors were mixed together until it turned murky gray. She turns to Billie, who all the while has been busy readjusting a stubborn glove. Hey, Billie, she says, this is a friend of mine, from the university.

Hello. The girl shines her eyes in his direction.

Hey Billie, he says and kneels down in front of her. He reaches with his hand to caress her curls. Suddenly his head is spinning and his breathing halts.

Hey, hon, a deep voice rumbles from across the road. They turn to see a tall, thin man, a bit hunched over, walking toward them, leaning on a wooden cane. Honey, Nina calls and waves.

Daddy, the girl cries out. She glides toward him, but as she comes near him she slows down and moves to hug him carefully.

Sunshine, he says, my sunshine.

Don't mess this up, Nina whispers to the psychologist, her voice quivering.

The thin man and the girl approach them. The men look at each other. Nina introduces him, a friend from grad school. The thin man stretches out his hand and the psychologist shakes it.

Yes, he says, years gone by. I'm in town — he looks around him — actually for the first time, at the hospital here; there's a conference, a workshop actually, the psychology of decision making or something of that sort.

Sounds boring, Nina says.

Depends on the decisions, I suppose, the psychologist says. Either way, I got out for a short break, to walk around town after three hours of sitting, and suddenly, well, what do you know? Small world, as they say. I heard this familiar laughter, it's hard to mistake that laughter, and — indeed.

How many years have passed? Four, five? You haven't changed, Nina says.

Neither have you, but I see that some things have changed. He motions toward the girl.

Nina hugs her, smiling: Yes, and you?

I'm not there yet.

How did the physiotherapy go? Nina turns to her husband.

All right. He manages an achy smile. Physiotherapy, he nods to the psychologist. Sometimes the repair is more painful than the breakdown. That's how it is with the body. How is it with you guys, with the soul?

The psychologist chuckles: With us it's not always clear what's the repair and what's the breakdown. They smile.

We're on our way to dinner; would you care to join us? the husband says.

Yes, Nina says, why not?

The psychologist looks at her, hesitates for a second. No thanks, he says finally, really, thanks, but I have to get moving. There's a summary meeting at the hospital and then the long drive home. But it was nice to meet you.

Take my number, Nina says, handing him a gold business card. If you're in town again, call me.

Sure, he says. Thanks. Bye now.

Bye Billie, he turns to the girl.

Bye, she says.

He turns and walks away. After a while he stops, turns back and looks after them, three figures walking away, wrapped in their heavy coats, moving slowly up the hill toward the parking lot, Billie's hand in Nina's. And then he sees Nina turning her head back toward him. From where he stands he cannot see her eyes, and her face too is blurry due to the distance. A small whitish stain remains, and then it too disappears.

On the way back home his gut seems to collapse inside him. The softness of the girl's curls lingers on his fingers. A cloud of disquiet gathers over him. A wound has been torn open, he thinks, and the bleeding has begun. Evening is falling, and his car tears through the mounting darkness, gulping the yellow dividing line with its headlights. He feels light-headed and dizzy. He grips the wheel tightly. Where are your feet right now? he mumbles to himself; breathe, relax your muscles, let your thoughts float by like autumn clouds, let them glide by. Observe without holding on. Her curls, such silky softness; a tiny rotund bear cub in a shiny red coat. The light in her eyes; let go, surf your emotions. What have you done? What brought you here today? Where is this used car headed? He must have scared her. She must

217

be frightened, and rightly so; such an invasion, desperate, impudent, how could she not be alarmed? And her alarm will surely seep into the girl's consciousness; without a doubt it will leak through; everything leaks. Then again, excitement; a flame of arousal must have been lit inside Nina. Surely she was excited to see him like this, out of context, abruptly, unexpectedly, as it was in the beginning, as it is in all beginnings before it fades and slips and evaporates; the piercing lightning in the gut, the craving, the impulse to shatter the basins of reality; the drunken freedom of beginnings, which is the child's gaze, the child's electrified curiosity. Surely all these stirred in her depths, too; the yearning and the unruly tides. Don't say I feel such and such, he always tells his clients; say a part of me feels such and such; because there is always another part, the quiet eye of the storm. And the antithesis is always present; because we are afraid of our desires and desire our fears. And Nina too must feel the tinge, the stinging and sweet bite; she too surely wakes up sometimes in the middle of the night tangled in a web of dread. She sees herself years from now, chained to her husband's sickbed, trying in vain to scrape against the incessant crawl of his illness's rust, to maintain his fading body. She too once in a while must look up to the sky, over the lush treetops and the herds of white sheep clouds floating about the endless blue meadow. She too wonders and longs. She too is tired. Do the right thing, the right thing, the right thing until you no longer can remember what the thing is and what is right about it. Until the boundaries fade, as they do for the traveler in these endless fields, when the depths of the open horizon, without a mountain or the shadow of a mountain, invade and tangle in the traveler's gaze and slip silently into his blood and throughout his body and consciousness until for one moment the traveler himself turns into an endless field with no here or there, no movement except the whispering wind and light and darkness. Yes, he has made a promise and a vow; but he is not naive and no longer innocent. Day after day he sees in that little room the march of humanity, fully clothed and yet naked. Day by day he sees the clay jars of promises break, their contents spilling to the ground in their myriad colors and scents, and the pieces then turn to dust from which new jars will be fashioned, and so on and so forth tomorrow and for eternity, and who will dare object? Who shall stand and admonish? Who can claim to have cracked the code?

His car gallops now, the headlights swallow the dividing line. He zigs and zags among the trucks, hulking beasts to his car's sprightly panther. My child. My child. Her amber curls, silk and light; the bells of her laughter. Mine. From me; my seed, my flesh and blood. Billie. His temples throb. He breathes heavily. He pulls over at the side of the highway. Giant trucks barrel by like the cars of an endless train, splashing through the filthy mud, sending rattles through the body of his car as they pass. He crumples in his seat, places both hands on the steering wheel, and rests his heavy head on his hands. Where are your feet right now? Autumn clouds, crisp, transparent air.

A piercing squeal is heard outside, a siren. He sits up, wipes his eyes with the back of his hand. A police car stops behind him with a heavy grunt. He sits still, his hands on the wheel. He feels at once embarrassed and relieved. He's not afraid. He has not broken any laws, and aching thoughts are not yet reason enough to arrest someone. He rolls down his window. The policeman, heavyset and thick-armed in pressed uniform, ambles slowly and stands as policemen do, just a bit behind him by the window.

Any problems? His voice, soft and polite, belies his whalelike presence.

No, no, the psychologist says. I just had to stop for a few minutes. Headache.

Well, sir, the polite whale says, you are not allowed to stop by the side of the highway. Do you know that?

Yes, of course. I just stopped for a few minutes . . .

An accident can happen within a few seconds, sir. No stopping on the shoulders.

My mistake, the psychologist says, I wasn't thinking there for a moment.

If you're tired, you should stop and rest in one of the rest stops along the highway. There's one just two miles down the road, sir.

I understand. Will do.

The whale pauses for a long moment. The psychologist sees him leaning, pointing his flashlight through the passenger window into the backseat. You're good to go, sir. Drive safely, he says finally.

The psychologist rolls his car slowly on the highway's shoulder, speeds up gradually, and rejoins the flow. His head, he notices, is clear now, and the muscles in his body have settled and relaxed. Something about the policeman's presence, paternal and direct, calmed the psychologist down. Don't get carried away, he thinks, take your time. Have perspective. Don't try to eat the whole apple in one bite. One slice at a time.

In the afternoon he sits in his campus office, laboring to grade a pile of student papers. There's a knock on the door.

Yes, he barks, straightening slowly in his chair.

Jennifer walks in, hugging a stack of books to her chest; her gaze is downcast. You wanted to see me, Professor?

Yes, he nods, please have a seat. He motions to the chair. She sits down, curled around her books.

You are a talented student, he says. Very talented. I think it's important that you develop habits that will improve your ability to express your talents, rather than habits that will hinder you.

She hangs her eyes on him in silent query.

The last two weeks you've been showing up late to class, or not at all, he says.

I know, she says, straightening up in her chair. There's stress at home . . . her voice trembles and cracks; she swallows and falls silent. Tears arrive. She tries to hold them back, clenches her jaw, and presses her books to her chest.

He waits.

You don't have to explain yourself to me, he says finally. I just wanted you to know that I've noticed. And that I am willing . . . I want to help as much as I can.

He pauses and waits.

I'm stuck, she says suddenly. Something happened to me. You see, Professor, I, from a young age I have always known, I was clear about my goals. I'm an only child. My parents barely graduated high school. But they worked hard to provide for me, to give me a chance. I was always good at school. I always brought home good grades. All A's. As a child I remember my father used to tell my mom, we're raising a doctor here, an astronaut, and he was all beaming. He used to lift me up in his arms and fly me through the air. To the moon, to the moon, he used to shout. In high school I took AP classes. I was a cheerleader. I was on the student council. I wanted to go to a large university but my parents insisted that I go here, close to home. And I understand them. I understood them. In high school I met Justin. Jennifer and Justin, everybody says, you were born for each other. Even your names match. He was an athlete. A star. He had admirers wall to wall, but he chose me. After three dates he told me I was the love of his life. And me too, I wanted him. I love him. We fit perfectly together. He had a younger brother who died in Iraq. It affected him. He had to grow up fast. Immediately after that we agreed to get married. He took me in his pickup truck to the lakeshore — she holds out her hand — and gave me this ring. It's a real diamond. I said yes, of course. I was on cloud nine. And now we are planning our wedding. He wants a big wedding. Big love, big wedding, that's what he says. After high school he joined his father's business, in construction. His father is going to retire someday and Justin will take over. I will graduate and become an elementary school teacher. I've always loved children. He wants four children. Big love, big family, he says. We already picked out names: Josephine or Jody for a girl, Jack or Jimmy for a boy. It's funny, we planned ahead so much, and we haven't even had sex yet. I was ready, but he insisted we wait. Strong love, strong discipline, that's what he says.

I understand, the psychologist says. And the last two weeks, the tardiness?

Ah, lately, yes, suddenly I have anxiety attacks. Suddenly I started thinking, you know, what are you doing? You are a child. You haven't seen anything; you haven't done anything yet. I feel like I'm on a bike going downhill. I pedaled fast and it was fun in the beginning, but suddenly the fun has been replaced with terror, maybe not completely replaced but mixed with it, and it's like I can't stop. I don't even know if I want to stop, though. And your class, something happened to me there; I started thinking . . . I feel things. It's not like other classes. You see, even this bike metaphor, where does it come from? I don't think in this way usually, I'm all business, feet on the ground. But look, I've learned. There was a moment . . . her voice trails off.

A moment, he says.

Do you remember mentioning in class a writer, Wasser, something like that?

Robert Walser.

Yes, that's it. You told the story how an admirer of his found him in a mental hospital and asked him why he didn't write and he said, I'm not here to write; I'm here to be mad.

Yes, I remember. We brought it up in class in the context of our discussion of the inner voice . . .

I don't remember the lecture well; I mean I took notes, of course, but that line, it did something to me. It stuck in my head, I don't know why, and you don't like the question why, but it didn't let me go. I started thinking, why are you here? It was always clear to me. Because the voices around me were clear, and I followed the expectations, you know, because that's your home, your strength, and I always understood the rules. I accepted the rules easily; but the inner voice . . . her voice unstitches and evaporates. She gathers herself and straightens in her chair. I'm babbling and you're probably busy. I'm sorry; I'll show up on time from now on. I won't disappoint you.

Let's not worry about me here, he says, let's focus on you.

Yes, yes.

Look Jennifer, he leans toward her: I understand what you are going through. Not completely, but I hear the music. And I don't have advice, you know from our class discussions. Just one thing: this crisis you are experiencing is not a crisis, it's a gift. Whatever happens, whatever you decide to do, that's a separate issue. But this moment of self-reflection is important in and of itself. It's a gift you gave yourself.

She wipes off a tear. Thank you, she says. Thank you for taking the time to listen.

It's an honor, he says, and one more thing, may I ask a personal question?

Sure, yes.

Do you cut? He moves his fingers up his forearm.

She looks at him surprised. There is a pause. How did you know?

I could see.

I cover my arms. I'm always in long sleeves.

That's what I saw.

I only started recently, she says, honest.

He nods. As your teacher, I cannot get too involved in your private life, and I don't know much about you. But I know this: cutting won't bury the pain. And the pain, the doubts and fears, these are things you can address in therapy. You don't have to carry everything alone. Nobody can carry their entire burden alone.

You're a psychologist. Can you treat me?

He shakes his head: No. You are my student, and we're not allowed a dual relationship. But I could recommend someone if you wish . . .

Thanks, she says abruptly, I'll think about it. She gets up and collects her books to her chest. When she reaches the door she turns toward him. I have an answer for you, she says.

An answer?

Yes. The story with the bird in Holland that toppled the dominoes and got shot? You asked what it was about.

Yes.

I know what it was about. It's a story you can break down and analyze and find analogies and lessons in it, and then it becomes a story about life. But you can also experience it whole, and then it's not a story about life. Then it is life. She turns and leaves.

A week goes by and no word from Nina. The psychologist sits in his office at the Center for Anxiety Disorders and anxiety gnaws at his center. He checks his e-mail. Nothing. He stares at the phone, pleading and encouraging. Nothing. He feels suddenly like he's descending a creaky flight of stairs into a darkened basement. Of course she's angry, as he violated his vow, tarnished their agreement, destroyed the delicate balance, cracked the thin shell with such recklessness, let himself go for a moment. Let what go? A yearning; he let himself ascend into the open sky of longing and now he's out of fuel; now the doomed plane is falling back to earth in a smoky spiral. Hold tight to your seat cushion, he tells himself bitterly, hold it tight, you fool, and prepare for an emergency landing. Here are the oxygen masks dangling in front of your face; passengers with children should put the masks first on themselves and then on their children. Billie's ringing laughter sounds in his ear, her silky curls, the almond eyes; he's short of breath. He sits up in his chair, places one hand on his stomach and the other on his chest. Take a deep breath, he tells himself, through the diaphragm. The hand on his chest stays in place while that on his stomach rises as he inhales. Correct breathing. Step-by-step, inch gingerly back from the edge of the cliff. Now think clearly. You failed. There is no doubt. And what of it? A person is bound to falter here and there, and in the long run, who knows? A butterfly in Africa, a hurricane in Australia. You hurt her, but she is resilient. Don't patronize. She will take care of herself. And what of you? Who will take care of you? He gets up and paces around the room. I will wait. Give her space, he thinks. Be patient and calm. Perhaps nothing has happened; a temporary setback; a forgivable stumble. We will work through this and return to the old order. I will wait. But underneath this layer of calculation another movement gathers, darkened, its chin pointed, rising and bubbling to the surface of his consciousness. Billie, my child, I am coming; your daddy, your father is on his way.

He calls Nina.

Hello?

Nina, it's me.

Momentary frozen silence.

Yes.

How are you?

OK. I'm busy right now.
We need to talk.

The hiss of static on the phone line.

Nina?
I'm busy right now.
I'll try you next week.
Yes, bye. She hangs up.
He's taken aback, leans back in his chair, rubbing his forehead with his hand; he gets up and grabs his coat and goes out to walk the streets. His mind is scattered and numb. He walks past the deserted car wash, descends the few stairs and strolls around the new shopping center that is materializing gradually in layers of steel and sheets of glass. The air is frozen and sealed. The psychologist walks down the steps to the cement walkway that hugs the curves of the frozen river. In the summer months the place is filled with strolling families, couples hugging, children feeding the ducks on the pond; the winds swoosh the leaves of the trees, the frogs crackle under the water lilies, fish slide in their silent world. But now everything is empty and still and covered with snow. The psychologist walks fast; his boots crush the pavement ice. The noonday sun peeks out feebly through the stained curtain of clouds.

He shoves his hands in his pockets and wanders about aimlessly, as if the cold has frozen his mind. He walks back to the street and arrives at a small bar. An unlit neon sign hangs lopsidedly on the front door. He pushes open the door and enters. The place is empty. A faded pool table stands in the corner. Behind the bar stoops a smallish man, craggy and ponytailed, busy drying glasses with a white cloth. The man looks at him with a friendly half smile. The psychologist approaches the bar, rubs his hands together and blows into them.

Cold, he says.

Winter, the barman says.

Wanna play? The psychologist asks him suddenly, gesturing toward the pool table.

I'm working, not playing, the man says.

The psychologist nods. He pays for a rack, takes it over and sets it on the table. He grabs a pool cue, scrapes some chalk on the tip, and leans over the table. He hits the balls one by one into the pockets. He walks around the table, observes and calculates angles, approaches, paths. The barman watches him from his station behind the bar, sensing anger's faint shadow in the visitor's determined pacing around the table. One ball after another falls into the pockets with a dry click and sigh. Finally only the white cue ball is left and the black eight ball in the opposite corner. The psychologist bends over behind the cue ball, taking final aim. He hears a rustle at his side. He looks up and sees the barman standing there with a knowing smile. The barman puts a bottle of beer on the small table nearby, nods and says, this one is on the house. Then he examines the pool table and says, everything about pool is geometry, except the last ball. He taps his temple with his index finger: That last ball, that's psychology.

Tonight we'll remember Gordon Allport, who was born nearby, in this American Midwest, among the corn and soybean fields that surround us as well, the psychologist says. They tell a story about young Gordon, who decided on his way back from a year of teaching English in Istanbul to stop in Vienna, and managed to arrange a meeting with Freud himself. Allport entered gingerly into the old master's office. Freud sat across from the young man, watching him and waiting silently, as was his custom. Allport, young and eager and as such not comfortable in silence, decided to try some small talk and proceeded to describe to the old analyst an episode from earlier in the day. On the train, a small boy, perhaps four years old, was traveling with his mother. The boy seemed wary of dirt and kept telling his mother, I don't want to sit here; it's dirty; don't let this dirty man sit by me. Everything was dirt to him. The boy's mother, Allport observed, seemed to be a proper, domineering and stern woman, and the connection between her and her boy's behavior seemed obvious.

When he finished, Freud looked at him intently with his famous piercing eyes and asked, and was that little boy you?

That encounter led Allport to conclude that Freud-immersed as he was in the lives of his patients, in their neuroses and defenses and unconscious motives — had neglected the surface. In his effort to uncover the hidden he had misplaced the obvious. Deep psychology, Allport observed, is often too deep, and in that sentiment he expressed, ironically, a deep insight. One of Allport's main contributions to our work is a principle that helps us understand one of therapy's biggest pitfalls. This is the principle of the functional autonomy of motives. It expresses a simple truth: what caused a process to begin is not necessarily what keeps it going. For instance, the reasons you started smoking — to impress the girls and rebel against your parents — are not the reasons you are still smoking at age fifty, when the parents are dead and the girls are no longer impressed at all. What caused you to get married is not what keeps you married. The young psychologist seeks the source of the client's problems and believes that if he finds the source, he has solved the problem. As a child you were attacked by a vicious dog; that's why you are terrified of dogs today. End of story. Well, not really. The fearsome dog of your childhood explains how your fear of dogs commenced, but not why you are still afraid all these years later, when you are no longer a child and that dog is no longer around. Your childhood story explained your childhood reactions, but not your present reactions. What can explain your present reactions, Jennifer?

The present reaction, ah, if I understand correctly, she says with hesitation, continues over the years because of avoidance. The girl who started fearing dogs continues to fear them because she is avoiding them. The encounter with the dog began the fear, but the avoidance of dogs maintains it, because she cannot relearn, learn from today's reality . . .

Indeed, the psychologist says, well said. And this leads us to our next business of the day: the false tyranny of childhood. This fundamental maxim, that the child is the father of the man, as Wordsworth said, is a blight on psychology and an obstacle in therapy. This idea, fundamental to Freud and his followers, crystallized, we must remember, in a certain historical time, during the late nineteenth century, when women of the emerging European middle class found themselves suddenly with time on their hands; when the barriers between the classes had become malleable and the possibility of climbing or falling down the social ladder became real and palpable, rendering the enterprise of child rearing suddenly important to the future of the family, and making it also a respectable pastime and an anchor in the midst of stormy social upheaval. And the notion survived to this day, where on TV the fallen celebrity du jour is always justifying his latest misbehavior by confessing some childhood sorrow to audience applause and nods of empathy. And right now still somewhere in America a worried mother is busy playing classical music to her sleepy infant girl to help her brain develop, lest she fall behind her peers, lest the scaffolds that surround her splendid emerging future weaken and collapse, lest that sleepy girl begin to harbor ill feelings toward Mom for neglect. And all this commotion seeps and invades the therapy room, where both the psychologist and the client have convinced themselves that the key to now is in the distant past, and the more distant the past the greater its power. Like a fantasy of a foreign land, far away and hence exotic and alluring, childhood too tempts us to seek in it the keys to our present-day turmoil.

The psychologist stops, takes a deep breath, and leans against the computer desk.

The class stares at him silently.

So what are you saying, the pink-haired girl asks finally, that childhood is not important?

Important, yes. Decisive, no. Informative, yes. Determinative, no. And here the good psychologist must be doubly cautious, because the client is bound to walk into the office already loaded with this particular narrative: the key to my trouble *now* lies in my experiences *then*. And the temptation is great to give the client what he wants, support his assumptions, and buttress his worldview, which is after all a psychological world-view. But let me ask you a simple question: if a loving childhood, a calm childhood filled with mother love and stimulating play is the key to a healthy character and a good life, how come all around the world children are raised in a thousand different ways — in poverty or wealth; with or without spanking; with or without siblings; in a city or a village or a boarding-house or a commune or an orphanage; in small or large families; some in rooms filled with toys and some in mud huts where chickens scratch; in skyscrapers or igloos; wrapped tight in blankets and left in a quiet room, or smothered and spoiled endlessly; in the care of elders here and in the care of siblings there — and somehow the vast majority of them, despite the differences in circumstance and custom, grow up to be normal and happy and functioning within the context of their cultures? They will talk at age two and at seven will participate in household chores and mature on time and slide into the stream of life smoothly and without calamity. And how will you explain, on the other hand, history's murderous march? The rape of Nanking; the horrors of Mao and Stalin; the Cambodian genocide and the genocides in Bosnia and Rwanda. Germany in the forties and Darfur today. How will you explain those millions of people turning overnight or over a short decade into murderous beasts who devour their own neighbors and friends, with whom they only yesterday sat and laughed and played and vacationed and shared a culture, a language, a future? Are you going to say that all these people had bad childhoods? The neighbor who turned thief and scammer and cold-blooded killer, who turns a blind eye to the plight of his victims, wasn't he loved by his mother? Wasn't he the apple of her eye? Didn't she caress him and bathe him and wrap him in soft blankets? And the torturer who hanged his victims from a hook in the ceiling, who sent a child to his parents with his eyes torn out, didn't his mother love him and sing sweet lullabies to him and tickle his ribs and breast-feed him and hug him in her warm arms? And the murderer who throws an infant in the air and skewers it with his knife in howls of wicked laughter in front of the pleading mother, didn't he play tag with his father in the yard? Didn't he pet his puppy years ago, speaking to it sweetly? What are you going to say? Will you claim that all of these were rejected by their parents? That the parents cursed at them all and neglected them all throughout their childhoods? Who will dare make such a claim?

A tense silence descends on the classroom.

★ ★ ★

Wow, Professor, Eric says, you feel strongly about this.

The psychologist breathes deeply. Gone are the smiles of the white teeth girls.

Something in your childhood? Eric says.

The students laugh uncomfortably, but the psychologist, lost to a sudden inner swirl, does not notice. His eyes wander to the window. A dry branch rattles in the wind outside, slapping against the glass, hitting it ferociously and then settling, leaning in and caressing it. The psychologist freezes suddenly, his breath halts and a sharp lightning pulsates through his stomach. His head spins. But he steps forward and gathers himself. Beyond my outburst here, he says quietly, this you must take in. The human architecture — our habits and customs and the molds of our souls — that architecture is constructed over time in a never-ending process; a process that does not end at five or fifteen or fifty or ninety-five. And there is no designer. There is no executive. There is no one in charge. Many forces collaborate and compete in this project, and declaring any one of them superior is incorrect. And the alchemy by which these forces of design interact is mostly unknown, which is why the psychologist, who walks in this deep dark forest, will do well to possess a generous measure of humility and reverence.

Nathan tugs at his tie; he clears his throat and raises his hand. I believe, he says, in my opinion, and without judging anybody, that there is someone in charge. There is God. And I don't dismiss what you have said. But as I see it, there is, like, a geology of the universe, like layers. And above your layer of no God, that maybe works like you described, like the layer of earth and trees and animals, there is a God, in the upper layer of wind and sky.

In the afternoon the piano tuner, a heavyset, droopy-eyed Asian, shows up at his apartment. He ambles in, and behind him plods his son, a pencil-thin, square-jawed youth whose eyes, peeking from behind the black curtain of his hair, suggest that he's been dragged here against his will. The piano tuner crosses the living room and approaches the sleepy piano. He lifts the cover, bends down and plunks a few jumpy notes on the wounded keys. His face contorts scornfully. He turns to the psychologist. Where did you find this piano, he asks in a sharp and impatient voice, on the street?

In truth, yes, the psychologist says.

The Asian's tortured face takes on a note of surprise. He nods slowly. Useless junk, he adjudicates, you shouldn't waste the money.

How much will it cost me to get it to play? the psychologist insists politely.

The piano tuner stares him down with cold contempt. It'll be cheaper for you to bring a truck and take it to the junkyard, he says decisively. He lifts the board that covers the piano's hammers and strings, looks inside, reaches in with his hand to feel something, pokes his finger and retreats in pain, sucking his injured finger, cursing in an unknown language. For who? Who will play this piano? You have children?

No, not for children. For me, the psychologist says.

You play? The Asian measures him up and down, and then looks around in desperation. With the money you'll spend fixing this you can buy a new piano, or almost new. This one's a hundred years old, and even a hundred years ago it wasn't very good.

I want to tune this piano, the psychologist says calmly.

The piano tuner sighs: If you insist. Eight hundred dollars, I'll make it play. More than that I cannot promise. But I will make it play, like a piano.

Agreed, the psychologist says.

Half the money now, half when the job is done, the piano tuner says.

I'll write a check, the psychologist says.

Cash, says the piano tuner.

Cash, repeats the psychologist, nodding.

The piano tuner motions to his son, who was leaning all the while against the wall, his headphones covering his ears. The son straightens up; his eyes are angry and sad. He rolls his headphones into his coat pocket.

They approach the piano together. The father removes the front board and looks inside over the keys. He barks instructions in his mysterious language. He kneels down on his knees, leans forward, and removes the lower board. He fumbles behind the pedals, waving aside thick spiderwebs. He takes a huge screwdriver and a heavy hammer out of his toolbox, leans in and shoves them inside the piano's entrails like a midwife. Squeaks and moans emerge. The psychologist shudders for a moment but then senses a strange excitement rising in him. Some old screw is turning in there, reluctant and recalcitrant. The piano tuner rises and calls his son to come over. He points with suspicious excitement at some place inside the piano and bursts out laughing, and it is clear that he sees something in there that his son refuses or doesn't know how to see. The piano tuner barks his orders, and the boy, slack and awkward, turns to obey them and goes out to the car; his father looks after him and shakes his head from side to side. The boy returns, carrying with him several mysterious tools, an immense pair of pliers and a banged-up can of oil. The piano tuner commands him, and the boy hands over the tools one by one like a surgeon's assistant. The piano wakes up suddenly and groans loudly, shrieks and

244

rattles. The piano tuner bends over it, sweaty and grave. He takes a deep breath, and the psychologist senses that a crucial moment is at hand. The piano too must have sensed that, and it begins to grumble and protest with an angry echo. The piano tuner bites his lips, leans forward, and then a sudden push, a tug and a lift, and the piano's guts are pulled out all at once, like a skeleton from inside the body. The psychologist watches with amazement, sees the hollow body, and then looks at the piano tuner who's already bending over the moldy keys, removing them swiftly and arranging them in rows on a piece of newspaper he has spread on the floor, numbering them with a pen. The boy returns to his headphones and stares out the window. The piano tuner folds his newspapers carefully and collects his tools. He barks at his son and the boy picks up the piano's naked skeleton and walks out to the truck. The psychologist stands before the vandalized piano, caresses it with a merciful look. He looks into the hollow of the piano's body, robbed and defiled like a pharaoh's grave. A multitude of emotions churn within him but he cannot name or order them. The piano tuner returns inside, wipes his forehead with a dirty cloth. His son remains in the truck, slumped in the passenger's seat looking bewildered and bored.

Wow, the psychologist sighs.

You got a vacuum? the piano tuner asks.

Vacuum? Oh, a vacuum cleaner, yes. He goes to the kitchen and returns dragging behind him a corpulent vacuum cleaner. The piano tuner takes the vacuum pipe, shoves it into the piano's cavernous body, pushing and poking around the silent corpse. At last he stops, turns off the vacuum cleaner, wipes his brow, replaces the front boards and mumbles something to himself in his secret tongue. Then he turns to the psychologist. The money, he says, rubbing together his thumb and index finger.

Ah, yes, of course. The psychologist goes to his bedroom and returns with an envelope filled with cash. The piano tuner counts carefully, humming an obscure pentatonic tune. He shrugs his shoulders, stuffs the money into his pocket, picks up the wrapped piano keys and says, I'll be back in three weeks. Be patient.

The psychologist nods; his eyes follow the piano tuner as he leaves.

What does it mean to be precise? This question occupies the psychologist's mind tonight as he sits in his small office at home, where he prepares his lectures. Is the therapist like a classical musician, who's focused on the sheet music and seeks to grasp the spirit of the piece as the composer envisioned it? Or should we view him more as a jazz musician, who seeks spontaneous, immediate personal expression above all? A black desktop lamp lights his old wooden desk. His toes dig into the carpet. Where are your feet right now? he likes to ask his clients as he leads them through correct breathing and body awareness exercises. Perhaps precision is a sort of accurate movement, like sharpening a pencil — those who insist on a perfect tip will continue to sharpen until the pencil disappears altogether. Einstein said, make everything as simple as possible, but not simpler. Perhaps beyond some thin, slippery line, the attempt to be precise, to see with clarity, turns into a futile quest. And if so, then what's left? What exists in the gap between possible and perfect knowledge? This question dissolves slowly in his mind and satisfies him. He gets up and walks over to the kitchen to make himself a cup of tea.

The doorbell rings. The psychologist straightens up with some surprise. Who's here at this hour? He walks to the door, opens it and sees the four o'clock client standing there. Her hair is wild; she's quivering, hugging and rubbing her shoulders. Angry rain falls behind her, pounding on the scarred pavement. Her makeup is smeared. High heels. His eyes take in the scene as they stand there, quiet for a moment.

What brings you here at this late hour? he asks finally, strangely calm given the time and the fact that his client has breached protocol and tracked him down at his home.

I don't know, she mumbles, and we're not in the office so I can say it.

He waits.

You said you'd help me, she mumbles.

I will help you as a professional, not as a private person.

Her pleading stare peels off a layer of haughtiness that wraps his answer, revealing, he thinks, a grave error at its core.

He knows about Michelle.

He? Who?

Bora. He knows about my daughter. He threatened me.

You need to go to the police.

The police, she snickers, and tell them what? That he's got a video of me blowing someone backstage and he'll give it to the judge if I don't come back to dance and the judge will say I'm an unfit mother? The police . . . she sighs and tosses a lock of hair from her forehead. I can't take it anymore, she cries. How much more . . . She coughs. He smells alcohol on her breath.

You are scared, he says. You are feeling confused and frustrated. I can see that. You are in a difficult place. But you have been in difficult situations before and you have overcome. And you will overcome this too. This too shall pass. We can process it all in session. Are you thinking about hurting yourself?

I rub men's dicks through their pants, she says coldly. Does that look like self-love to you?

Are you thinking about suicide?

She is silent for a moment: Yes.

Do you intend to kill yourself?

No. I won't leave my child an orphan.

Have you ever attempted suicide?

No.

Do you have a weapon at home, a stash of pills?

No, no.

Can you hold it together until tomorrow? We can meet at four, an emergency meeting.

Yes, she whispers.

I'll see you tomorrow at four, then, he says, his voice rising unwittingly.

She retreats slowly without turning around, wavering on her high heels. He watches her from his doorway. She turns and walks away. He steps onto the porch. The wind slaps the trees, whips around dead leaves. He sees her walking down the street. Where is her car? he wonders. How did she get here? Where is she going? He thinks he should go after her, but on second thought he decides against it.

He returns to the kitchen. His tea is cold. He puts the cup in the microwave and waits. He leans on the counter, his head down. This is not the first time a crazed client has shown up at his doorstep, but it's been many years since it last happened. In fact it hasn't happened since he stopped seeing borderline clients and turned to focus on anxiety clients, a shift in direction he chose to undertake because the question of fear is the most fundamental — here, he thinks, Freud was right — and also because anxiety clients are not usually afflicted with psychosis or stupidity, two conditions that science has yet to resolve. Anxiety clients keep their boundaries and play by the rules and tend to get better in a short time. And there's satisfaction in that. The treatment of personality disorders, on the other hand, tends to stretch out indefinitely. Every week brings with it a new crisis that both replaces and complicates the previous one. And deep inside, clients with personality disorders believe that there is nothing wrong with them; that the source of their problem resides in the mean, chaotic or indifferent world: the authorities, the neighbors, family members.

This surprise visit from the four o'clock client disquiets him. Before he goes to sleep he walks through the house, locks the doors and closes the curtains. Something about Tiffany's eyes, her gait, has penetrated his shell. He acted professionally and ethically, of that he's quite certain, but the sight of her wobbly figure disappearing in the sheets of rain has shaken him.

The shutters rattle in his dream. He wakes up at once and stares at the ceiling. Outside, the wind blows through the empty street, swirling around the bare treetops. His apartment moans and creaks. The wooden floor squeaks. The dining room chairs, heavy and obedient beasts of burden, crowd around the table trough. The apartment is alive. Everything is alive, in its own way. He lies on his back, laces his fingers behind his neck and studies the shadows on the ceiling. Dawn will soon break, he thinks, forever fresh, magical. Suddenly panic. Cold panic envelops him. His breath halts and a sickening realization hits him: Bora did not know about the girl. He, the psychologist, has betrayed her. He, in his zeal to turn back the sleazy crook, to protect Tiffany, in his prattle about her rights and her wishes, has leaked the idea of a secret; he gave Bora the hint, a clue that Tiffany may value something above herself. Betrayed Tiffany and betrayed his code. And what now?

He lies in bed for hours afterward, tossing and turning. He hits his head on his pillow and curses at the air. He tries to sleep but can't. He chases after sleep but wakefulness, sour and sharp, chases him. He stares at the alarm clock until it rings.

Tiffany sits across from him in the clinic office. Her eyes are swollen and red from crying and lack of sleep. Without makeup, her skin appears gray; her clothes hang loose on her thin shoulders. She searches nervously through her bag and pulls out a cigarette and a lighter. She lights up and inhales deeply. He sits quietly. She crosses her legs, sets her elbow on her knee, and looks at him, then at her cigarette, and again at him.

He waits.

Aren't you going to say anything? Your rules?

Last night you showed up at my place very upset. You said something about Bora and the girl. I want to understand exactly what is going on, the psychologist says matter-of-factly.

She falls silent and seems surprised at his sternness. He threatened me, she says. Yesterday, the way he does, that snake, you saw him — she drags from her cigarette. He said: Maybe you can fool your shrink but you can't fool me. You can't fool Bora. I smell something. I took care of you; I set you up nice. I watch over you. You won't run away from me so fast. I stood up to him. You know, this time . . . the things we talked about here, it came to me; I'm a person, a human being, a full person, not half person, not subperson. I survived. I'm not a slave. I have rights. I told him to his face: I'm not your slave, I got rights, you made money off me, every night you made money off me; I'm sick, I told him, I'm not a machine. Suddenly I went crazy in my head; I started yelling, you know, throwing things. I told him he can't hold me. If I want to leave I will . . . he can't hold me. I'm not in prison. A few of the girls came to hold me back. He came over and whispered to me: I know about the girl. And I have stuff on you. A judge sees what I have on you, you think you get custody? If you want to see your girl, you will need to be smart. You need to do business with me, yes? She weeps softly. That snake, she says. I was careful. How did he find out? He must have spied on me.

The psychologist leans toward her. First, I am happy for you, he says.

Happy?

The decision to stand up to him, to demand your rights, was the right move, a positive and brave decision.

254

It wasn't really a decision; I went crazy.

We decide to go crazy too, he says, in some ways. You expressed a healthy impulse there.

Much good came out of that . . .

We will examine the result separately from the process. A healthy process has value unto itself, regardless of the outcome. A healthy process does not guarantee a good outcome, but it enables it. An unhealthy process contaminates every outcome. If you achieve something through lying and cheating, your cheating contaminates your gain, annihilates it, really. If you earned it fair and square, then what you got is truly yours. And even if you got nothing, your integrity itself is an achievement.

I have to get Michelle back.

At any price?

At any price.

Let's look at the facts. Are you sure he has incriminating evidence on you?

I don't know, probably. In the beginning a few times I slipped, I was addicted, customers came in, you understand, Doctor . . .

Please be precise.

I got paid for oral sex. Blow jobs. Is that precise enough for you? Did he videotape it? He said he did. I can't say for sure. It's not above him. Nothing is above him.

And what's next?

I need money. I have to dance. In a year I'll have enough. I have a plan, Doctor. I'm not dumb. But now . . . that snake . . . she covers her face in her hands, I don't know.

★ ★ ★

After the session, after Tiffany leaves, the psychologist remains sitting in his office. His stomach churns. He leans back in his chair and contemplates his dilemma: should he confess or not? On one hand, it's not imperative that she learns how Bora came to know about her daughter. And it's unlikely that Bora himself will say something. And even if he does, the psychologist could deny it, and she'll likely believe him. The question before him, before them, is how to manage the new situation. Will it benefit her to know that he is the source of the leak? This information will only complicate her feelings toward him. It's likely she'll become angry. Perhaps she'll project her helplessness and anger onto him, blame him for her failure to retrieve the girl. Perhaps she'll decide in a storm of emotion to end treatment altogether. Perhaps she'll file a complaint against him with the local board; professional malpractice, disclosing confidential information without the client's consent, a serious transgression that requires inquiry, which may leave a mark, a blight on his record and reputation. It is legitimate for the psychologist to protect himself and his good name, especially if such defense also coincides with the client's interests, and is it not in her interest to continue therapy with him? In an atmosphere of trust that they have built? After the road they have already traveled? In light of her emerging self-awareness and empowerment? Is it correct to sacrifice this concrete process that is still at its core healthy and productive in the name of total disclosure of some truth, the concealment of which will not detract at all from the process within which it was revealed?

Here he needs Nina's help. He puts his hand on the phone and he freezes. They haven't really spoken since that hallucinatory visit, since he drove there and revealed himself to her, supposedly by accident. Go tell that to Freud and his troops. She hasn't called since; nothing by e-mail. But here we're talking about a professional issue. And the client's future, perhaps also his professional future, both are in the balance. Surely they are able to separate the professional relationship, still fruitful and intact, from the personal one that's been tarnished and soiled. He calls her. A voice says: I'm not at my desk.

Please leave a message. I will get back to you shortly. He hesitates for a second and then says: Hey, it's me. I need a consult regarding the stripper case. It's urgent. Strictly business. I won't talk about the other stuff. Call me. Please.

Tonight we will examine several known therapeutic obstacles, the psychologist says. First is what we may call *interpretive exuberance*. The beginner therapist, excited to have been handed the tools of interpretation and the authority to deploy them, will always tend toward excessive use. Like a new driver, like a new recruit holding his rifle for the first time, the young psychologist eagerly seeks an opportunity to use the power that has been bestowed upon him; to demonstrate his skill. Suppose you have in front of you an anxious client. One frozen snowy morning a few months previously, on his way to work, the client's car slid on an icy highway bridge, bounced off the rails, rolled over and came to a stop, luckily in the median. Since that day the client has been reluctant to drive to work in general, and in particular he's loath to drive over bridges. He has developed a paralyzing phobia. How will we treat him?

Exposure treatment, Jennifer says. He needs to practice driving over bridges many times. We can start with a small bridge on a country road and progress slowly . . .

Very good; and the psychologist?

The psychologist will chaperone the client. You said that the psychologist is allowed to accompany the client in exposure tasks. We can take him to the elevator in a high-rise if he has elevator phobia or fear of heights. We can take him to the zoo if he's afraid of snakes. We need to support him, like scaffolding, you said . . .

Correct, the psychologist says. A well-planned sortie into the client's day-to-day life, for observation or to support a therapeutic exercise, is often required and welcomed. Here too we may all benefit from shedding the constraining Victorian legacy of the mighty Viennese. For example, regarding our case in point, we will want to accompany our bridge-phobic client to the bridge. And why is that?

As he drives over the bridge we can help him, Jennifer says, remind him to breathe. Remind him to check his inner speech, dispute irrational thoughts; remind him to go with the flow of emotion, that negative emotions are not always a bad thing, and not the end of the world. We can ask him periodically about his anxiety level and record his progress to see if his anxiety subsides. Like you said, repeated exposure leads to habituation of the nervous system, and when the nervous system activity is reduced, anxiety is also reduced.

Indeed, the psychologist says, that's all right and sound, but also incomplete. What's missing? What other reason do we have to want to accompany the client?

Jennifer bites her lip and turns to rifle through her notes.

Silence. The psychologist looks around the room; he lifts his hands. Nathan sits upright, staring vacantly forward. The girls with the white teeth smile politely. The pink-haired girl glances sideways at Eric.

To see if he can drive, Eric announces suddenly. Maybe he's just a lousy driver and rolled over because of that, and then he should stay home and off the highway, or maybe learn to drive before he goes out in the middle of winter to do exposure treatments . . .

Yes, the psychologist smiles, indeed. The expert always wants the right answers to reside in his area of expertise. But our area of expertise is of no interest to the right answers.

As someone who rides bikes, Eric continues, I'm telling you that bad drivers are my worst fear.

Jennifer rolls her eyes and sighs into her notebook.

The psychologist smiles: Let us return, if you will, from the wild highway to our business at hand. He motions to Eric. What is the business at hand?

Interpretive exuberance, Jennifer chimes in.

Yes. The young psychologist, as I said, feels under pressure, since he senses the client's expectations; since he has to justify his fee and his long years of apprenticeship and study. This is why he seeks to force the interpretation hammer upon the client's unsuspecting head. Here's another example: a young client sits in front of you telling you her story, and as she speaks she periodically lifts her hand to cover her mouth. What does this gesture mean? He looks around. To whom exuberance? To whom interpretation?

The Freudians will say she's scared at the unconscious level of exposing some incriminating information, Jennifer says. She's resisting; she's ambivalent.

Yes; and what will the cognitivists say?

They will ask her what she's telling herself, what she is thinking.

Yes; and the behaviorists?

Learned habits, Jennifer says. Maybe in the past she used to spit as she spoke and got ridiculed for it, so she learned to cover her mouth.

Indeed, a nice application of the behaviorist credo. Someone is listening here. Hallelujah, Jennifer; you have warmed my old, tired heart.

And what will the humanists say, apropos the heart?

Ah, I'm not sure; I don't understand them that well.

No, of course not, the psychologist smiles; nobody understands the humanists, and that includes the humanists themselves. They are difficult to summarize. To them, the attempt to summarize is itself a vainglorious effort at reductionism, which is contradictory to the subtlety and nuance of the existential experience. He walks toward Jennifer. And what do you say? How will you interpret the client's gesture?

She hesitates: I don't know enough yet.

Maybe she ate onion soup for lunch, Eric wakes up in the back, and her breath smells bad, so she covers her mouth.

Nice, the psychologist says. Our friend Eric refuses to yield to the tyranny of theory, refuses to fall in the trap, and that's important, unless of course he does so because he does not know the theory, because he tends to fall asleep during lectures . . .

Ouch, Eric says, clutching his hand to his chest. That hurt, Professor.

You're a robust specimen, the psychologist says. You'll survive, I have no doubt. But let's get back to our business. What then is our next move? Whom shall we trust, Freud or Eric?

263

Freud, Jennifer says.

Me, Eric says. The pink-haired girl nods to herself approvingly.

Nathan raises his hand slowly: With your permission, Professor, and with all due respect, I will decline both options. Both of these are merely mortals, lost sheep. I will trust only my Lord and Savior . . .

Neither Freud nor Eric, I agree, the psychologist says, but for different reasons. You dismiss my two alternatives because of a sense of certainty that emerges out of faith and requires only faith to sustain it. I will dismiss Freud and Eric too, but I'll do so because of a lack of certainty. How come? Eric?

I don't know. But ouch.

Funny. How come, Jennifer?

Ahh, evidence?

Evidence?

You always say that scientific knowledge is based on evidence. You say we have to let the banana ripen even if we are starving, because if we pick it too soon, we won't be able to eat it anyway.

And what do I mean when I say that?

Ah, you want me to explain what you mean, to *you*?

Isn't the psychologist charged with explaining to others their own intentions?

You mean it's wrong to jump to conclusions;

we need to wait, look for converging evidence, and seek patterns, not anecdotes . . .

Nice job, Jennifer. The good psychologist needs to provide the client with a long enough rope so that the client can in due course help the psychologist out of the pit of his own illusions and theories. Freud did famously say, even a cigar is sometimes just a cigar; and Albert Ellis did say, there is such a thing as irrational rationality. And Confucius did say, everything in moderation. And I say, yes, let go and wait. The cigar is always just a cigar and a phallic symbol. Things are complex, and absorbing this complexity takes time. In jazz they say you need to learn everything about your instrument, and then learn everything about the music, and then forget both and just play. Absorbing the complexity, that's the task. Imagine that you happen upon a construction site. You see three people breaking rocks. You ask them what they are doing. The first one says, I'm breaking rocks. The second one says, I'm making a living. The third one says, I'm building the city. Well, who's telling the truth?

All three? the pink-haired girl says hesitantly.

But how is that possible? They are saying different things.

Each one comes from a different perspective, Jennifer says.

Yes, and that's the fundamental quality of the human experience, that it is always multi-dimensional, at once concrete and universal, at once partial and whole, one thing and everything. We can give this idea a verbal expression. Try this exercise: switch all your daily *buts* with *ands*. Jennifer — he turns to her — instead of telling your fiancé, I love you *but* you're driving me mad, tell him, I love you *and* you are driving me mad.

She curls into her chair. We don't usually say those kinds of things, she mumbles.

I want to buy a new bike, Eric says, *and* I have no money.

Now, the psychologist says, don't you feel better?

I feel better *and* I still have no money, Eric says.

In his mailbox, which he shares with three other adjunct professors whom he has never met, he finds a stiff white envelope decorated with delicate etchings of flowers. An invitation to Jennifer's wedding. He turns it over and contemplates it; Jennifer, hmm; he tosses the envelope into the trash absent-mindedly and turns to walk to his office, but then he stops, turns back, fishes the envelope out of the basket and takes it with him. The phone rings. He hurries to his desk and picks it up.

Hey, it's me, Nina says. Her voice is measured, but not icy and distracted as it was the last time he heard it.

Thanks for calling me back, he says. His heart rejoices.

I committed to help you on this case. I honor my commitments, she says sharply. What's the situation?

He tells her.

Are you sure that her boss, that Bora, actually found out about the child through you?

I rambled about her plans and wishes that maybe extend beyond herself; and he seemed quick, and I seem to remember he registered a response; at the time I didn't realize what it meant ... I think he put two and two together, and Tiffany showed up at my apartment a short while afterward. Chronologically it makes sense, and also by my intuition, and I don't have much more to go on. I'm not going to ask him ...

OK, let's assume you slipped somehow. What now?

If you were in my shoes, what would you do?

She thinks for a minute. I would have acted by the same principle that guides my decisions as a mother, she says.

Which is?

Get to know your child closely and intimately and then act based on that knowledge; let go of abstractions and theories.

He is silent. His stomach hurts.

I didn't mean to hurt you or mix up things, she says quietly. I just want to help.

I know. You have helped. Thanks, you're free to go.

OK, bye.

Yes, bye.

Tiffany sits down and the psychologist says: I need to discuss an important issue with you related to our therapy. I think your boss, Bora, learned about Michelle from me; my slip of the tongue.

Slip of the tongue? What do you mean? How . . . when? How did you get to talk about Michelle?

We didn't talk about her directly, but when we met here in the clinic, he said he was suspicious that you were not sick, that you were looking for a way out. I said we were working on a real problem and that your future plans were not my concern and that you had the right to do what you wished with your life and think beyond the present, beyond yourself even. I'm afraid he may have caught that hint and that led him to check on you.

When did you realize this? she asks, her forehead creased.

Two weeks ago.

Why didn't you tell me?

I wanted time to think and decide how to respond, what would be correct for the treatment, what move would be most helpful for you; and I also thought about myself, about the risk of admitting a professional mistake.

And why did you decide to tell me?

I decided that you had the right to know the truth about what happened and about me in that context, so you can decide on your next step while knowing all the facts.

She looks at him, severe and hunched over; she tugs at a lock of hair that curls at her temple. Her legs are crossed and the one on top shakes continuously up and down; suddenly it stops. Thanks, she says.

Thanks?

Yes. You hurt me, Doctor; you messed me up with this. But I feel that you wouldn't have told me about it, you wouldn't confess if you didn't trust me, if you didn't have trust, if you didn't care about me. Her shoulders quiver. Tears. A gift, she says quietly. I feel you gave me a gift. I won't disappoint you. From behind the curtain of tears a smile emerges, merciful and knowing, the likes of which he has not seen on her face before.

He nods. I understand, he says, and I appreciate your sentiment, and at the same time it is important for me to remind you that our business here is not me but you. If you disappoint me or not, this is not a concern you need to have. Your decisions must be based on your interests, your needs, your values and goals. You need not bother yourself with me. I can take care of myself. You don't have to protect me.

I know, she says. I don't have to. I choose to.

A week later Nina calls. Thanks for not overreacting last week when we talked, she says.

Thanks for returning my call. It helped me.

What did you decide?

I told her.

And her response?

Good. She took it as a sign of my trust in her. A certain closure, you could say.

You acted correctly, with moral courage.

By the test of results, for now it seems so. In the long run, who knows?

In the long run we're all dead. That's your line, is it not?

So you do listen.

We need to talk about what happened.

Yes.

Face-to-face.

Agreed.

Midway between us there's a small town, Bloomville; one light, one gas station. I'll meet you there for lunch.

Unlike the Hilton.

Completely different.

I'll be there.

If you want to get back on stage, he says to Tiffany, you will have to confront your fear in real time.

In real time?

Yes. You've practiced at home. You know that the symptoms of anxiety in your body are scary but not dangerous. Now you have to face your fear straight up. The only way to overcome anxiety, you already know, is to break through it. Evasion and trickery and suppression and distraction will not work. You have to accept your fear, embrace it, face it and confront it head-on. Right now your problem is not fear, but your relationship to fear. You are still afraid of your fear. You think that in order for you to dance again you will need to stop feeling anxious, but the truth is that in order to dance again you will need to manage fear, not get rid of it. None of us ever gets rid of fear. But we can learn to manage fear correctly, react to it properly, live with it peacefully, and even use it to our advantage.

I don't get it.

I'll give you an example. Imagine you're in the ocean, and the waves are quite large, quite

273

scary. What will you do? You can get out of the water, but then you won't be able to enjoy the ocean. And then the fear controls your life. You are a slave to fear. It determines what you will do. And if you internalize this kind of solution — avoidance, withdrawal — as your pattern of dealing with fear, then you know what will happen: your life will become a story of withdrawal, continuous defeat in the face of fear, and the more you lose the stronger fear becomes and the weaker you become. In addition, avoidance prevents learning.

I still don't understand.

If you don't spend time in the water, you'll never learn to swim. Fear, in its deepest meaning, announces the need to go forward, not the need to retreat.

OK, so I stay in the water.

Correct move; but not sufficient. Your behavior while in the water is also important. You can try to stand up to a big wave, stop it with your body. This attempt is futile and dangerous. The wave will bury you.

I can dive and let it pass over me.

Better. More effective, but not much fun.

OK, you're fishing for something, I see.

Fishing, yes, nice, he smiles. For what?

I don't know.

We have . . .

Yes, yes, our rules. What to do with the wave? Don't run out and don't dive under . . . I need a boat, a submarine . . .

Don't distract yourself. You're in the ocean, here comes the wave . . .

Ah, surfing! she calls out victoriously. I can ride the wave. She stands up suddenly, one foot before the other, her hands spread out as if balancing on an invisible board. Ride it, she says, ride it!

Tiffany, the psychologist says.

She halts, straightens her shirt with her hand and retreats back onto the sofa.

Sorry, I got swept away, she says.

He waits quietly.

Swept away, get it?

He smiles: You're scared to go back to the club.

Yes.

And what am I going to say now?

About what?

About the fact that you are scared.

You are going to say: Very good. It's an opportunity.

An opportunity for what?

To practice.

What?

Confronting my fear. To manage fear correctly.

Right.

And now what?

Next week you're going on stage to dance.

At the club?

Yes.

I'm ... I ... I'm not ready, I'm not sure ...

You are telling yourself that you are not ready. What is this thought?

A guess, an hypothesis.

Right, and what do we do with those?

Test them.

Right. You know how to dance and you know about fear and what you need to do about it. That's the evidence.

I'm scared.

Great. Good. You are a human being with human emotions, and without waves how will you ever learn to surf?

And what about you?

It depends. If you want to do this by yourself, that's OK. If you feel my presence will be helpful, I will be there. The most important thing is to commit to face your fear. No retreat. You cannot go back on this. Once you give your word, you are committed. Whatever happens, you must go through with it. Whatever happens will be useful data for us; everything except retreat. If you're going to do it, you have to make a commitment.

Scary, she says.

Scary is just a word. Milk milk milk milk, he says.

She smiles: Milk milk milk milk.

Promise.

I promise you. I'll dance.

Don't promise me, promise yourself.

I promise myself.

OK. It's set.

And you?

Me?

Will you come?

If my presence helps . . .

It will help.

I'll be there.

Noon. He waits at the gas station in Bloomville. An enthusiastic radio host rambles on about the weather. The psychologist is in good spirits since he is about to see her soon. Her image in his mind, her neck, her lips, crowds out his knowledge of the circumstances of this meeting. She will soon be here. He drums on the steering wheel absentmindedly and looks in the rearview mirror, runs his hand through his hair. A white sedan glides by and he sits up alert. He turns and sees an old man at the driver's seat and beside him a small boy in a baseball cap, his hand poking out the open car window, painting twisted lines into the wind. The psychologist takes a newspaper from the backseat and settles in to peruse it. Last week's sports news is no longer news, he thinks, except to those who haven't read it. His eyes linger on a picture of a young female tennis player in a short white skirt, her knees slightly bent, her back arched backward, her racket raised in one hand and the other stretched up, palms open; her eyes look up, following perhaps the flight of the ball somewhere outside the frame. Her floating white figure, reaching for the sky, seems pure and dreamy to him. Dreams, said Havelock Ellis, are real while they last. Can we say any more about life? The game is a dream, the psychologist thinks. As long as it lasts, the players and spectators are invested in it completely; when it is over, they rush to read about it, to validate their own experience, to break the narrow circle of the internal monologue and widen it to include the world, and also to check whether someone else saw something they did not. Perhaps someone's description will crack some secret code or mix the familiar ingredients into a new stew, finer and richer than before.

He hears a honk nearby. Nina sits in her Subaru, motioning to him with her hand to follow her. He nods, tosses the paper in the backseat, and the two cars glide down the street to a small restaurant. They park in the back, side by side. He gets out of his car and walks over to her.

Hey, she says, her face severe. Let's go inside.

He walks behind her. His previous giddiness, he notices, has morphed into an anxious stomach churn. They enter the restaurant and sit at a square corner table in the back. She orders salad and a glass of water.

Aren't you eating? she says.

Suddenly I'm not hungry.

I'll get straight to the point, she says, I don't have much time.

She doesn't have time, he thinks. She needs to get back to collect Billie from day care. This thought spreads in his brain like a rust stain. He squirms in his chair uncomfortably.

I want you to explain to me what that was, that episode.

I wish I knew, he says. I'm assuming there were many reasons blended together. I wanted to see Billie.

Suddenly, just like that?

Maybe. I thought . . . before you leave . . . one time.

Was that the first time?

Yes, yes.

She looks at him suspiciously.

I'm not lying to you. I've never lied to you, he says.

Her salad arrives and she pushes aside the plate.

Recently things are shifting for me, he says. Suddenly I'm aware . . . I see children around, at the college, at the clinic, things bubble up . . . his voice scatters like smoke. His throat is dry. He drinks from his water glass and his voice returns: I didn't mean to hurt you or Billie.

Let's be straight with each other, she says. I need clarity here. You see, I'm raising Billie.

I am in a certain situation. I cannot look over my shoulder every day. We didn't think about it then, and until you showed up I didn't think about it at all, really; but since then I am in turmoil, I've lost my peace of mind. Her face reddens and her voice cracks: I don't have sound legal footing here. You can sue for paternity any time, you can shatter everything . . .

No, no — he leans toward her, anxious and offended at once — I've never thought about doing that. I don't think that way. You know me. Look at me, it's me.

Years have passed, she says. Do we know each other? How much do you know anyone, really?

He is taken aback; her suspicion seeps into him, engulfs him, becomes a part of him.

And what about me? he says suddenly. What about me? All day I'm everyone's daddy, the students, the clients; and my own daughter . . . His voice breaks, he tears up, he wipes his eyes with the back of his hand, a move he's seen a thousand times in his clinic. I feel real yearning, his voice rises, and it comes from a clean place — he hits his chest with his hand — and you react as if I'm a snake in the bushes. Look at me, put yourself in my shoes; at night I see ghosts, I hear voices. He chokes: It's not a crime, you know, not a crime; she's mine too, my blood, isn't she? You can't push me out. I promised, yes, but what of it? Who will judge me? And you, what are you really about? What is your agenda? Didn't you put my hand on your breast? Who are you anymore? Why did you give up, really? Why?

She is silent.

Tears.

You're right, she says suddenly.

He leans back, confused, unsure which of his myriad claims warranted this judgment.

I didn't act correctly, she says. It's not your fault. And I want you to know — she leans toward him, wipes her cheek — I will never fight you. I will always see you as my lover, never as my enemy. And I am not running away. I'm moving to try to help my husband. My husband is very sick. Do you understand?

He sits in silence.

She gets up and shoulders her purse: I need to go now; you will act as you feel is right. Just think about Billie. She takes a few steps toward the door, and then she stops and turns to him. Just think about your daughter.

She pushes the door and goes out.

Don't go, he whispers, and then he says, OK, I'll pay.

He inhales deeply, and as he exhales, even before his lungs have emptied and his hands have risen to hold his head, he knows he has given up.

The psychologist remains at his apartment this morning, awaiting the piano tuner. At eleven the piano tuner shows up, his son dragging behind him. The piano tuner carries the piano's old guts, now clean and tight. He enters the living room, kneels to the floor and opens his rolled newspaper, inside which the keys gleam in shining virginal white, begging to be touched. The piano tuner hums to himself joyfully, caresses and arranges his tools in a row on the floor. His joy, the joy of a craftsman at his craft, radiates around the room, absorbs into the carpet, cheers up the dwindling plant on the windowsill, but bounces off his son, who's crouching solemnly in the corner. The piano tuner approaches the piano, wipes it with his cloth, opens the cover and fiddles under it. He calls his son over in an excited voice. The son nods feebly. The piano tuner looks at him with pleading, desperate eyes. His shoulders stoop and he returns to his labor. The psychologist retreats into the kitchen, clears the stage for their dance.

Something to drink? he calls out.

Just water for me, the piano tuner says. The boy is silent. The psychologist pours a glass of cold water and puts it on the bookshelf in the living room. The piano tuner is busy with his resuscitation efforts; he walks around the piano, touching and measuring. The psychologist retires to his office and sits at the computer. Within a few hours, sounds begin to emanate from the living room, pure, precise notes. First a trickle, then a flow and then a flood. He walks into the living room. The piano tuner sits at the piano; his wide back is hunched over the shiny keys, his thick stubby fingers dance around vigorously. Merciful sounds spring forth from the depths of the old piano. The piano tuner raises his head and looks sideways and up, as if searching for a certain point in the ceiling or in the invisible sky beyond it. His face beams; his eyes now close. His son leans against the wall, staring out the window, expressionless. The piano tuner stops suddenly and gets up from the stool.

The best I can do, he says. His eyes flicker and turn off. The best this piano can do. The psychologist hands him the envelope. The piano tuner opens it and fingers the bills. He seems suddenly exhausted and terrified, as if he has aged all at once. He calls his son over to collect the tools. The son wavers, mumbles something under his breath and then drags himself over. The piano tuner follows him with his eyes; he sighs heavily. His eyes float about and land on the psychologist and for a brief moment a kind of silent plea flickers in them, a silent note of bottomless sorrow appears and disappears, and the piano tuner straightens up and turns to leave.

Thank you, the psychologist says. The piano tuner turns and nods with a slight bow and goes out without a word.

From the parking lot of the Silver Fox club, which is half filled with beat-up pickup trucks, you can see the lights of the landing strips that end just over the airport fence. The psychologist parks his car at the edge of the lot and slips out of his seat. A huge airplane swooshes overhead like a spectacular, giant bird. The building itself is low and square; small red lights flicker around the roof, trying and failing to add glamour to the desolate scene. As he steps inside, a dense darkness hits him. The music too hits him, heavy pulses of a deep bass, urging, demanding. He gathers himself and tries to assume a nonchalant, knowing air as he scans the room. Busy colorful lights throb all about a narrow elongated stage at the front of the room. Several girls, in various stages of undress, are gyrating to the music around three shiny brass poles. A mishmash of men is scattered on the chairs and sofas: a herd of eager, slaphappy students; several bands of middle-aged men who stopped here on their way home from work, sitting defeated in their crumpled suits and undone ties; a few tourists who got stuck on their way to a bigger and more important city; assorted street eccentrics, wild-eyed and drunk. He walks in, locates an empty table by the corner of the stage and sits down. A tiny Asian waitress appears from the darkness and bends to yell questions in his ear. He orders a beer and she disappears into the commotion behind him. Boff-boff-boff, the ceaseless bass thumps in his ear, stirring the dense air and rattling the inside of his skull. The psychologist looks at the stage. Around the nearest pole a black woman is whirling lazily; her skin shines and her eyes are blank. She spins around the pole in her high heels and then grabs it with both hands, face to the ceiling, arches her back, turns and falls to her knees, spreads her legs and slides her finger slowly up one leg. She brings her finger to her lips and then again down between her legs and then she crawls to the edge of the stage and stretches out her finger toward one of the spectators, a trembling, heavyset man who leans forward and draws out his neck as if to lick her finger. She brings her finger close, waves it in front of him, flutters it down his face; he leans in and then she suddenly arches back on both hands, twists her pelvis and grabs hold of the man's face with her thighs, like the jaws of a wild animal. In his left hand the man is waving a five-dollar bill, like a flag. His head disappears between her generous thighs; her hips wriggle and move slowly up and down; she takes his hand in hers and leads it to her thong and stuffs the bill in it. And then her thighs yield and open and she slides back, turns and gets up and shimmies off the stage without looking back, leaving the man at the foot of the stage behind her, yelling, hollering, waving his hands; and then he falls down into his chair, woozy and exhausted.

The psychologist is also woozy and exhausted for a moment. The waitress materializes from behind him with a bottle of beer. He pays, sips, and looks around. The stage empties, the lights dim further, and a voice rises from somewhere, announcing in excitement, and now, please welcome back to the Silver Fox stage the sexy, the bewitching, the one and only, Tiffany Johnson! Yellow and red lights flood the stage and begin to throb; the bass returns, insistent and urgent; the audience claps and hoots, and out of a white cloud he sees Tiffany, the four o'clock client, materializing slowly on the stage. The psychologist leans forward to see; his heart pounds. She saunters slowly toward the center pole. She wears a short leather miniskirt and a short pink shiny jacket that only half conceals a frilly white bra underneath.

She walks to the pole and holds it with one hand; she turns her back to the audience and bends down deeply and slowly, her buttocks raised. She freezes and turns her head back toward the audience. Her stare hits the psychologist, at once childish and knowing, inviting and rebuffing, contemptuous and pleading. Now she turns, her back leaning against the pole; her hands are on her knees; she spreads her bent legs slowly, as if in effort, and immediately closes them again. A teasing half-smile rises on her red parted lips. She shakes her head side to side; her hair splashes over her face; she stands up and walks to the front of the stage with a measured, decisive step. She grabs the sides of her jacket, slips out of it with one quick wiggle, throws it onto the floor, twists and drops to her knees and with a swift, almost invisible motion her bra falls open and she cups her breasts in her hands. Her hips, shiny and lithe, gyrate slowly; her back arches, her eyes close; boff-boff-boff, the bass thumps; slowly her fingers begin their retreat to the side. Her face takes on a pained and pleasured expression. Her eyes are now on her body, following her hands, inch by inch her breasts are revealed; tiny, erect nipples. The psychologist stares at her in a mixture of awe and disbelief, straining to see in this naked gyrating woman under the lights the four o'clock client, the childish, timid waif. He seeks a clear sign that it is indeed her, but cannot find it. Except for her face, which the throbbing lights obscure and distort, he cannot find a sign. Suddenly he feels as if he's slipping down a steep icy ravine, searching with his hands for something to grab onto but still falling fast, waving and scratching. Who is this woman? What is the link between her and the teary girl at his office? She now moves up and down on the pole, slithering, as if her whole body is being kneaded by an invisible hand; her back and shoulders shimmy. Slowly, like a drop of water onto a thirsty mouth, she slides down the pole, her fingers caress her face, flutter over her lips, her neck, her breasts and thighs, and in between them. She reaches under her miniskirt, lifts the sides of her red thong with both thumbs and slowly removes it halfway, then she stops, bends her knees, her hands over her head, stirring through her hair, her hips and thighs shake and swing, unruly, elastic; her eyes are foggy, scanning the heaving room before her. Suddenly she gets up and sashays to the corner of the stage, turns and stands in front of him, her hands in her hair, her legs just slightly apart; her eyes pierce through him and she swirls and agitates and twirls; her body shakes; boff-boff-boff, the bass hammers, and so does the

291

psychologist's head. She drops all at once to her knees, crawls and arches and turns over, boff-boff. Her legs open and close and she brings them to her chest, and in one slow smooth motion she takes off her thong, tosses it at him, at his feet, onto the stained floor. She spreads her legs for a moment, right in front of him and then closes them at once, rises, turns, glides off the stage and disappears behind the heavy purple curtain.

The tiny waitress reappears at his side holding a champagne bottle. She stands erect by the table, holding the bottle with a practiced, steady hand covered in a towel; she turns and pops out the cork and pours him a tall glass. The psychologist looks at her, surprised. I didn't order champagne, he yells. The waitress motions with her hand to the other corner of the club, toward a round table, around which several buttoned-up men are sitting, their faces obscured. The owner sent it, she yells back.

He brings his mouth closer to her ear. Say thank you for me, he shouts. She nods without smiling, collects the empty beer bottle off the table, and retreats.

After midnight he stumbles through the parking lot. His ears are ringing and numb, as if covered by a heavy curtain. The outside silence hits him. He approaches his car.

Doctor, he hears a call behind him. He turns and sees Tiffany walking toward him, wrapped up in a long white fur coat, her hair collected at the back of her head, in her hand a burning cigarette.

Doctor, she says. She stands in front of him. Too close, he thinks.

They look at each other.

You did it, he says finally. You took the next step. You kept your word. You went onstage and you survived. It's an important step for you. How do you feel?

She shifts her weight from one foot to the other, brings the cigarette to her lips, inhales deeply: A part of me feels good. She turns her head to the side and exhales a cloud of smoke; she smiles slightly. Another part . . . maybe . . . doesn't feel anything.

He nods: Complex reaction to a complex situation. We can process all this in our next session.

Yes, she says. And then she adds, I didn't do it for me.

Not for you?

For you, she says.

A giant airplane roars overhead, piercing the silence that has engulfed them. She steps backward. Next Friday, she says, and then she turns and disappears inside the club.

What is our goal in therapy? What, in the final analysis, do we try to accomplish? The psychologist looks around the room.

Change and growth, Jennifer says finally.

Perhaps, the psychologist says, but not necessarily. Change and growth are useful yet limited metaphors. They do not encompass enough complexity and are easily damaged by the moths of clichés. All around you hear talk of change and growth, as these are fashionable terms. But change, it turns out, is contrary to our deep nature. Human systems are often designed to resist change and seek stability, and for a good reason. A completely open system, without mechanisms to sort and filter and manage influence, will not survive for long. Every living system protects itself by guarding its boundaries; so with the cell, the organ, the body and the psyche. Look around you: the media of human expression have changed a great deal over the centuries, from cave walls to tablets to paper to computer screen. But the stories related by these media, the basic themes, have remained remarkably the same. A man from ancient times, having landed in our midst today, would be quite surprised by your car, Eric. But he would have no problem understanding the concept of moving from point A to point B, which is in essence what your car is about.

The white teeth girls smile, exposing their white teeth. The psychologist's gaze flutters over them. The house of the soul, he says, is built in stone. Winds may howl through its windows; people will enter and exit through the doors; they will bring in a computer and haul out a typewriter. The sun will rise and burn, snow will fall, wild weeds will sprout through the cracks in the floor . . . and still the house's basic imprint will remain unchanged. What am I saying?

Deep psychological change is difficult, Jennifer says.

Yes, the psychologist mumbles, yes. And so we must move about with humility and care. The promises of salvation, the miracle formulas and vainglorious speeches we will leave to politicians and young lovers. We will not thoughtlessly pursue change and growth; not for their own sake, at least; not at any cost. We will not worship them. There are other worthy goals for therapy: perseverance, continuation, stability, surrender. Remember that in a social context, we psychologists are stabilizers, not subversives. We do not agitate and incite revolts but are charged with returning people back to proper alignment, to normalcy, to the bosom of the social consensus . . .

But who decides? Eric awakes. Who decides what is normal? And why is normal good anyway? It's not always good. Slavery used to be normal. So if a slave wants to run away, will the psychologist try to persuade him to stay?

And women once couldn't vote, Jennifer joins in. So if a woman is depressed because she has no rights, will the psychologist call her sick? Maybe society is sick.

The psychologist nods and smiles. Indeed, he says, difficult questions, and relevant always. Clearly at any given time all of us are blind and weak with regard to something. This obstacle has no remedy except awareness and inquiry, and persistence and courage. The good psychologist resides, in a known sense, on the hyphen between the culture and the individual, and from this stance he must constantly examine both. All the while he also observes himself, his system of meaning and values. This process of examination will reveal to him that no one formula can capture the whole of human experience. Therefore, with due respect to change and growth, we will do well to remember that *surrender* and *concession* are not bad words in the therapeutic space. Not every client seeks to reach the mountain-top. Some seek to descend the mountain safely . . .

But you said that metaphors with positive connotations are useful in therapy, Jennifer argues. *Growth*, for example, is a term with positive connotations.

Yes, the psychologist says, and still, if we phrase everything in positive terms the very notion of positivity loses its meaning. He raises his voice: Not everything is positive in life. There are negative things. Severed limbs do not grow back. This life in the final analysis is a chronic, and terminal, condition.

You know how to encourage and uplift, Professor, Eric says.

I am trying to describe things with precision. To cling to positivity at all costs hints at shallowness, a difficulty beholding the inner complexity. It is better to seek synthesis and balance; to behold the paradox: push and pull, give and take, fear and courage, life and death. Accurate movement in the internal space, that's our goal. His hands are raised now and his voice softens and fades to a whisper. Bonnard's yellow brush, he mumbles. His hand floats in the air holding an invisible paintbrush, moving slowly up and down, like a conductor presiding over an unseen orchestra. His eyes close: The gesture, the right move, the right word . . . He gathers himself and opens his eyes. As that old bastard Miles Davis once said, you have to play just one note: the right note. And he also said, don't fear mistakes. There are no mistakes.

Jennifer stops her studious writing and lifts her head, looking at him with a confused expression.

The psychologist moves toward her. OK, I got carried away, he says. Here, write this down. The goal of therapy is to provide the client with the tools to nurture and maintain psychological health. We help him practice the correct use of the tools: acceptance of emotions, rational examination of thoughts; to consciously confront erroneous patterns of response and embrace the flow of correct, healthy patterns.

Jennifer breathes a sigh of relief; her forehead relaxes but then is creased again. But how can you tell healthy from unhealthy response? she asks.

If the client stands on the tracks and a train is approaching, the client's emerging anxiety is a correct response, a piece of advice he'll do well to heed. The evidence quite strongly attests to the fact that a head-on encounter with a train is harmful. But if the client stands anxious in front of an elevator, then he must confront his fear, not obey it, because the dangers of the elevator are negligible and avoiding it will cause unnecessary misery. And, as Freud saw early on, there's enough real misery with which to contend in this life; no need to add any made-up stuff. Your mission, Jennifer, should you choose to accept it, is to find out whether the client's problem is a train or an elevator; and then your mission is to help the client step off railway tracks and enter elevators. How will you accomplish that? With humility, as we have said; with your alert and accepting yet uninvolved presence; with reflection and guidance — those are the ingredients.

He falls silent for a long moment and looks at the class. How tired I am, a thought rattles inside him like a gust of wind. He composes himself: And still it is important to remember that however fluent and aware and accepting you are, however illuminating and healing the therapeutic experience, still it won't suffice to move the client. One hour a week of battering against the walls cannot breach a fortress built over many long years. The lessons learned in session must be translated into everyday practice. The shape of one's life, in the final analysis, emerges from the sum of one's everydays.

Did you like the show? Tiffany asks.

I was happy for you, that you kept your promise and achieved your goal. You found your courage. That was good to see.

Yes, but did you enjoy the show?

Let's focus on you. Where are you?

She fiddles with a stray lock of hair, bites her lips: It's strange to sit here with you. Weird.

Weird.

After the show and all that . . . You're my psychologist. You saw me naked.

I saw you confronting your fears.

Her eyes meet his. I decided, she says suddenly. She leans forward; her face is lit up, her pupils wide. Her skin gives off the fresh scent of delicate soap.

Decided?

Yes. I'm quitting dancing. I enrolled in the community college. I'm going to start school, evening classes. I'll find a job waitressing or something. I called a lawyer. I'm going to start a new chapter. You were right. I have been fooling myself. You know, after that night at the club, something changed for me.

I danced, you saw me, but it wasn't the same as before. Suddenly everything looked dirty to me. I didn't feel the power. I couldn't go back to the place I'd been before. It was weird, like a fake flower that looks real but it isn't, and it really has nothing to do with a real flower. Do you know what I mean? Suddenly everything looked like plastic to me, the tables and chairs and curtains and the people and costumes and me too; plastic, everything plastic, colorful but dead. Everything was dead. I felt it in my gut. Suddenly I could, like, see myself from outside; I looked at all these people and I saw clearly. I don't need them. Like you said, a car with headlights doesn't have to depend on streetlights. That night I decided to leave. Put an end to it.

I see. And what are the risks involved in this decision?

Risks? I don't know. I don't care. There are risks in anything. Who knows what will happen? If Bora wants to screw me over, let him try. Let him go to the police. I'll fight him. You will testify for me, won't you? I have dirt on him too. I won't live in fear, not of him, not of my father, not of my memories, not of my mother-in-law the witch. Let them all come after me. I'll take on all of them. Live free or die, that's what I say. No apologies anymore. And I'm not scared. Fear is dead. You know when we started here we talked about how I behave like someone who doesn't care about herself, doesn't value herself as you say; and I think after I realized that I kept going and I came around, and suddenly now I like came back from the other side. Now I don't care about that because I have something more important to care about: Michelle, my baby. She won't spend her life with that witch and that drunken bastard. That's it. That's what's clear to me.

You sound up, full of energy, very decisive.

She nods: I woke up today all charged up; like I'm floating.

It's nice to see you like this, focused and determined, he says. And in order to make sure that your decisions will really serve your goals, to make real progress, you need to take the next step, which is?

She wiggles on the sofa: Which is? I don't understand.

Sometimes we decide to act in a certain way because the destination is attractive. Other times we just want to act, and we find a destination to justify that need.

Explain.

I want to know if you have examined your decision thoroughly from all directions.

From all directions? she winces. I don't

know all directions. I have one direction. She grabs her bag and fumbles in it urgently and takes out the picture of her girl. She holds the picture to him, shoves it in front of his face: That's my direction.

That's your motivation, and it is strong and worthy; and a strong motivation, like a strong light, can blind us . . .

She frowns: Why are you picking on me? Her voice hardens. At last I'm up, and you have to bring me down?

Do you feel I'm acting against you?

Yes, you're pulling me down.

Do you truly think I am acting here against you?

She hesitates.

Look at the evidence, our history here; look at my possible motivations. Is it likely that I wish here to harm you? To undermine you?

Ah, no.

So the fact that my words are hard to take is not proof that I have bad intentions?

No, I know, I shouldn't take it personally.

Yes. Sometimes what's in your way is not a roadblock but a street sign. Let's examine your reaction, then. He looks at her and perceives immediately that she is not with him. He falls silent.

She looks at the picture in her hand, she lifts and kisses it, and then she raises a gauzy stare at him and says with an apologetic smile, sorry, what did you say? I'm a bit distracted today.

He waits, he thinks, and then he says, how can I help you now?

I want you to be happy for me.

The psychologist sits at his campus office after class, correcting papers. He hears steps coming up the stairs and wonders, who's around here at this hour? The door opens and Bora steps in, wearing a gray suit and his shiny blue shoes. Behind him stands a burly middle-aged man with thick eyebrows. The psychologist looks at them, aghast.

Let me guess, Doctor, Bora says softly in his nasal voice as he steps into the office. The burly guy remains behind, leaning against the doorway, poking at his nails with a silver nail clipper. Your client, Tiffany, she didn't come the last two weeks, yes? Bora looks around the office.

I don't talk to strangers about my clients, the psychologist says. His skin begins to crawl, at once frozen and burning.

We are not strangers, Doctor. We know each other, yes?

I am busy at the moment.

This won't take long.

What do you want?

She disappeared.

Disappeared?

305

Got up and left, and took the girl with her. The girl, how do you know . . . ?

Bora tosses an acidic sideways glance in his direction. I know things about her, he says. I know her real name, yes? You didn't think Tiffany Johnson was her real name? And I know she ran away and took her girl with her. What I don't know is where she went. And I was thinking, Doctor, that maybe you could help me, yes? We both have the same interest, to see her safe. You don't want her to be a criminal, a fugitive, a kidnapper, yes? I thought maybe she contacted you. Maybe she said something . . .

She didn't say anything, the psychologist says. His voice acquires a slight pressed tremor and his stomach churns. I'm hearing about it for the first time here, from you.

Yes, yes. I thought you would say that; but you see, it's hard for me to know if you are telling the truth here. From the beginning you were — how we say? — hostile; I came to you politely, like a businessman, and you answer — how we say? — not polite. I don't know. I begin to think . . .

Hey, Professor, a loud baritone voice rumbles from the stairs. Bora stops and turns. Heavy steps are heard and then Eric's head pokes in, smiling. He steps forward and takes his thermos out of his book bag. Black coffee, like you wanted, Professor. He blinks slyly.

What? Oh, yes, of course, thanks. Did you put sugar in?

Two, as you like.

Eric turns to dig into his bag: I also wanted to use this opportunity to discuss some points in this chapter that we're reading. He turns, looks at Bora and his bruiser. I mean, if, if you're not busy . . .

No, no, they just stopped by for a moment. We just finished here. They're on their way out. Please have a seat. He motions to the chair.

Thanks for coming, he turns to Bora, and thanks for the information. We'll be in touch.

Bora looks at him for a moment, and then at the large youngster, measuring him up and down, like an expert tailor.

Yes, he says quietly, yes, we will be in touch. He turns to leave and then at the door he stops, turns around: I asked you to help her. Do you think you helped her? And then he walks out.

The psychologist releases a heavy sigh. His heart, he notices, is beating hard and fast in his chest. His skin is sweaty under his shirt.

Everything OK, Professor? Eric asks.

OK, yes, the psychologist mumbles distractedly. What are you doing here?

I passed by and I saw these two parking in front of the building and walking in. They didn't look right.

Right?

A few days ago they announced around the dorms that some computers had been stolen recently and we need to watch out, keep our eyes open. And these two . . . their car, Professor, that's not a faculty car, not an administrator's car either; surely not a student car. A black Cadillac? Give me a break, Professor. My father is a mechanic, I know something about who drives these cars, and when I came up, just seeing your face I knew something wasn't right.

My face?

Not exactly a poker face, Professor. Let's just say in Vegas you'd be broke in an hour . . . and I sit for hours looking at you every week. You pick up stuff about people, you know. I know my test scores are not — how should I put it? — Harvard-level, but that's because I don't really like to read. I don't like to study much. Actually I took this class just because I needed the hours and it fit my work schedule, you know. I'm not really into psychology. Helping people with their problems, that's not my thing. I like bikes, to work on old bikes, you know. Anyway, are you OK?

The psychologist nods: Yes, yes. These guys, there's some issue in the clinic, but it's OK now.

You sure?

Yes, yes.

Where are you parked?

In our lot; here at the back.

Come, I'll walk you to your car.

Thanks, but there's no need. You've helped enough, really.

So you'll give me an A in the class? He laughs.

I don't give the grade. You earn the grade. You'll get what you have earned.

I'm just kidding, Professor, Eric says. I earned my C+ with hard work and determination.

Yes, yes, the psychologist sighs, really, you should go home now. I'm all right. I don't need an escort.

No big deal, Professor, Eric says. I just want to make sure your car starts. Are you still driving that old thing?

The psychologist nods.

They walk together to the parking lot. The night is quiet and cool. The psychologist gets in the car and starts the engine. Eric leans down by the window. Are we going to see you at the wedding? he asks.

Wedding?

Jennifer, she invited the whole class. Didn't you get an invitation?

Ah, I'm not sure, actually maybe I did, yes, I put it in my office somewhere, I completely forgot.

You should come, Professor, Eric says, she'll be happy.

Ah, in principle I don't usually . . . well, we'll see. I'll think about it.

Don't think too much, Professor, just roll with it.

Afternoon. The psychologist sits at the piano in his living room and plays. His fingers, as if awakened from a long sleep, walk delicately across the shiny keys. A jazz melody sounds, soft and halting, rising to dance around the room. Don't play what's there, Miles Davis said, play what's not there.

Nina, a whisper dissolves inside his head, Nina.

He looks up. On the piano, in a dark wooden frame, stands a picture of a smiling little girl hugging a pink teddy bear. The psychologist hears a rustle outside the front door and recognizes the sound of the mailman, wrestling as usual with the rusted mailbox. He gets up and walks over to the door. He steps outside, and as he pulls out the stack of mail he notices a small brown box amid the usual advertising brochures, coupon books, and assorted solicitations. He goes in, tosses the rest of the mail onto the kitchen counter, and looks the box over. Who would send him a package? There is no return address, and his own address is scribbled on the box in a handwriting that looks familiar to him, although he cannot place it. He tears off the outer paper, opens the box and pulls out a small porcelain cow with dark spots on her white body and large pink udder. The psychologist studies it closely, turns it around in his hand. Moo, he whispers to himself, moo. He walks around his apartment to find a place for it. His eyes wander around the living room shelves, the kitchen counter, the windowsill in his office, the square end table by his bed. He returns to the living room, walks over to the piano and places the cow near the girl's picture. He steps back, looks at the arrangement, nods slightly, and sits back at the piano and plays. The notes rise, clear, effortless and spare from the depths of the old piano and for a moment his spirit rises with them, weightless and without bounds like sunlight. For a moment he's absorbed in something that feels to him like peace.

A call rises from the corner: Speech! Speech! The psychologist looks around, cursing the sudden bout of softheartedness that brought him here, into this crowded, teeming hall; to stand among the tables piled up with food; to sweat under these bright chandeliers, amid the heavy red curtains; to walk into this storm of sentiment, of shouted conversations and congratulations; to witness the mother's tears and the father's sweat; to look over these decked-out guests whose smiles seem like they were pasted to their faces forcefully and forgotten there; to hear the whines and cries of the troubled child, the hungry child, the tired child, the terrified child; to see Jennifer's wedding gown, a lavish cathedral within which she is all but lost; to hear her earnest words float over to cross the endless divide to her husband, who stands by her all packed into his tailored suit and looks at once older and younger than he is. The psychologist stares into the humming space and suddenly he's floating as if in a dream, and the sounds around him join and weave into a soft comforting quilt.

Speech! Speech! He gathers himself and

focuses his gaze with some effort. He notices Eric and the pink-haired girl bobbing in the corner, flushed with childish joy, their fingers poking in the air in his direction. Beside them, the white teeth girls clap and yelp. He sips urgently from his wineglass and looks around, confused. He catches Jennifer's eyes from her seat at the front table. She smiles and motions for him to come up. He senses himself, to his surprise, walking toward the small stage. He takes the microphone in his hand. Squeaks and screams emanate from the sound system. His lips are dry and his head spins. All around a sound emerges, chimes, clinks of silverware on glass; fairy bells ringing. The crowd quiets down.

For those of you who don't know me, which is all of you, he says, I was Jennifer's teacher this year. I don't have to tell you what grade she received.

A wave of knowing laughter swishes across the room like a gust of wind, cooling the psychologist's flushed face.

Toward the end of her career with us she was impatient to finish. I guess this is the way of the world: babies don't want to take a bath, children don't want to go to bed, and students want to leave the university. Those of us who are older, of course, view a good bath and a good night's sleep as two sublime pleasures that we wish we could prolong; and we would pay a lot of money to be able to return, even for a short while, to our youthful college days. But every generation I guess has to learn anew that the oven is hot. Anyway, one day in class Jennifer told me that she was tired of the university and wanted to start her life in the real world. I told her then as a lesson, and I will tell her now as a wish: everything is a university. For those who see clearly, everything is a university.

A soft, nodding hum rises from the crowd. They are in his hands. The psychologist looks around the room. A pleasant warm sensation settles in his body. In the sea of ties he recognizes suddenly Nathan's erect serious figure. He raises his glass in the boy's direction. Nathan raises his soda can, and a half smile flickers on his face. The psychologist turns to Jennifer. And one more thing, if I may, he says quietly. You always had the ability to listen to your teachers; and for a veteran teacher, or old and half dead in student parlance, any encounter with a student who listens is experienced as a miracle to be enjoyed and not examined too closely, lest it vanish like a mirage. But — he leans toward her; she shines like a white frozen torch — during this last semester I have discovered another more important talent in you: the ability to listen to

315

yourself. There, in my opinion, is where the real learning begins. Congratulations, Jennifer, and thank you all.

Applause; whistles sound from the corner. Eric is waving at him enthusiastically, the pink-haired girl bouncing at his side. The psychologist steps off the stage, works his way to Jennifer, hugs her carefully so as not to upset her attire and makeup, and kisses her on the cheek. The white teeth girls exult around them and squeak with delight. Eric shows up behind them, smiling broadly, the pink-haired girl on his arm.

Good speech, Professor, Eric says. You definitely got it.

I'm not sure what I got, but thanks for reminding me of the wedding.

Now we dance, Professor, Eric announces. He raises his beer bottle in the air. The pink-haired girl squeals and pulls him onto the dance floor. The white teeth girls rush to join them.

The psychologist nods: You, you dance; my time has come and gone. He follows them with his eyes until they disappear in the throbbing, bouncing crowd.

He feels a gentle tap on his shoulder. He turns to see Nathan standing there. They shake hands.

Interesting class, the boy says. I enjoyed it. You probably don't see it this way, but I believe you are doing sacred work in there.

The psychologist smiles: How did it . . . has your dilemma resolved itself? If I may ask.

Nathan's eyes light up. Ah, yes — he inches closer and leans into the psychologist's ear to overcome the loud music — I told my brother to wait. I begged him, but he didn't listen. He told Mom.

The psychologist nods: And her reaction?

You won't believe it, he says, running his hand over his tie. She said that she knew all along, that she just was waiting for him to accept it himself. Would you believe it?

The psychologist nods: Yes, I think I would. And then he turns and walks out into the warm night.

In his car on the way back to town a warm exhaustion spreads inside the psychologist's body. He yields to the old engine's soft hum. Gradually his fatigue overcomes him and his eyelids droop. He stops at a small gas station, slips out of his seat, stretches and walks into the store that is bathed in white light. A young woman sits behind the counter; her face is solemn and her hair is held back in a ponytail. On her right shoulder he sees a colorful tattoo of a bare-breasted sea nymph with some letters etched over her head. The psychologist walks around the store. He pours himself a cup of black coffee and takes a bar of dark chocolate. He approaches the counter, hugging the coffee cup with both his hands, sipping carefully.

Good evening, he says.

She rises from her chair slowly, puts aside a glossy tabloid.

That's it? she asks.

That's it, he says, digging into his pocket and pouring a pile of coins on the counter.

She turns lazily to fiddle with the cash register.

Long day? he asks.

I work the night shift, she says. I just started.

He nods: How do you stay awake?

Customers come in, they wake me up.

He leans over and looks at her tattoo. He points and reads aloud the words above it: *No Fear*.

No fear, he mumbles softly.

A gift from my boyfriend, she says.

Wedding plans? he asks.

She shakes her head: He left.

And the tattoo? He motions to her shoulder.

What about it? she says.

Doesn't it remind you of the bastard?

She is silent for a moment, and then she shakes her head again: It reminds me of myself, in love.

Of course, he says, his soul suddenly ascending toward her, of course. Good night.

He turns to leave. She remains silent; her eyes follow him as he leaves and then she goes back to her chair and picks up her magazine and the memory of their exchange fades from her mind.

The psychologist drives on down the winding highway. His eyes are wide open. His mind is pacified like a sleepy baby. His obedient heart beats slowly inside his chest. Darkness all around.

Acknowledgments

I want to thank my Israeli editor, Rana Werbin, my agent, Jennifer Joel, and my editor at Holt, Helen Atsma, for their friendship, support, and expertise and for their tireless joint effort on behalf of this book. I also wish to acknowledge the theorists and researchers whose ideas and formulations echo throughout this book. These include Alfred Adler, Gordon Allport, David Barlow, Edna Foa, Sigmund Freud, Harry Harlow, Steven Hayes, Jerome Kagan, Abraham Maslow, Paul Meehl, Robert Sapolsky, and Daniel Schacter. Finally, I wish to thank Mia Lewis, my partner in life and in writing, who has spent countless, often thankless hours editing, tweaking, polishing, sculpting, and nursing this text into shape. Without you this book would not have come to be.

We do hope that you have enjoyed reading this large print book.

Did you know that all of our titles are available for purchase?

We publish a wide range of high quality large print books including:
Romances, Mysteries, Classics
General Fiction
Non Fiction and Westerns

Special interest titles available in large print are:
The Little Oxford Dictionary
Music Book
Song Book
Hymn Book
Service Book

Also available from us courtesy of Oxford University Press:
Young Readers' Dictionary
(large print edition)
Young Readers' Thesaurus
(large print edition)

For further information or a free brochure, please contact us at:
Ulverscroft Large Print Books Ltd.,
The Green, Bradgate Road, Anstey,
Leicester, LE7 7FU, England.
Tel: **(00 44) 0116 236 4325**
Fax: **(00 44) 0116 234 0205**

Other titles published by
The House of Ulverscroft:

MR. MICAWBER DOWN UNDER

David Barry

The ever optimistic Mr Micawber bids a fond farewell to David Copperfield, taking his family to Australia, confident their lives will change for the better. However, florid language and optimism is not enough to survive the brash life of Melbourne in 1855. Visits from the bailiffs, rent arrears, and his daughter Emma's betrothal to his landlord's son, all complicate Micawber's life. However, when his son Wilkins introduces a young man with an ambiguous past, who also has designs on Emma, it becomes even more tangled. Micawber turns detective, but will the mystery he uncovers threaten even his optimism and integrity?

JUST ANOTHER DAY

Patricia Fawcett

Is Francesca making a mistake when she decides to buy her childhood home in Devon? Or could this help her to come to terms with something that has haunted her for years? Can she ever be rid of the guilt she feels for the accident to her brother, for which she feels responsible? Meanwhile, her meeting with her old friend Izzy brings things to a head, for she was present that day and knows the truth. But can Izzy and Gareth, the new man in Francesca's life, help her find a way to forgive herself at last and move on?

THIS BEAUTIFUL LIFE

Helen Schulman

The Bergamots' move up to the city goes
well. Richard gets consumed by his new
job and Liz, having given up her career,
plays mother to six-year-old Coco and
fifteen-year-old Jake. But when Jake,
unthinkingly, forwards a sexually explicit
email attachment sent to him by a young
girl, the Bergamots' comfortable middle-
class existence is over. Within hours, the
video clip is all over Jake's school, the city
— and the internet. Facing impossible
choices, what Richard and Liz do next
risks destroying everything: their marriage,
their daughter, their place in the community and Jake — the child they have set out
to protect.

LAZARUS IS DEAD

Richard Beard

Life, for Lazarus, is mostly good, until far away in Galilee his childhood best friend turns water into wine. Immediately, Lazarus falls ill. And with each subsequent miracle his health deteriorates. He tries everything in his power to make himself well. Except for calling on Jesus . . . Lazarus dies. Jesus weeps. But as Lazarus is about to find out, returning from the dead isn't easy. You think you want a second chance at life, but what do you do when you get it?

A FATHER FOR DAISY

Karen Abbott

Beatrice Rossall's future seems bleak when her father dies. She is left with Daisy, the four-month-old orphan in her care, homeless. But when a local mill owner offers her the position of housekeeper, she refuses because of the appalling conditions he imposes. Affronted, he makes sure no one else in the area will employ her. Bea's only option is to find Daisy's father, Mr Dearden, in the hope that he will accept his responsibilities. But when he denies all knowledge of the affair, Bea has no money and nowhere to go . . . until fate steps in and offers her a way out.